Tales of the Magical Spartans

Fred Stabley Jr.
Tim Staudt

Sports Publishing L.L.C.
www.sportspublishingllc.com

Director of production: Susan M. Moyer
Project manager: Jim Henehan
Dust jacket design: Kenneth J. O'Brien
Developmental editor: Kipp Wilfong
Copy editor: Cindy McNew

ISBN: 1-58261-424-5

Printed in the United States of America

Sports Publishing L.L.C.
www.sportspublishingllc.com

Every reasonable attempt was made to give proper photo credit. If there are any errors,
please notify the publisher and corrections will be made in subsequent editions.

This book is dedicated to Tim's brother, Greg, and our families.

Greg waged a gallant eight-month battle with brain cancer, which finally ended for him on March 7, 2003. He owned a boat marina with his wife Debbie in Venice, Florida, for some 20 years.

Greg grew up in East Lansing, and his wife graduated from Michigan State after attending Alma High School.

Greg attended Indiana University, but he was a Spartan through much of his life and was enthused about this book throughout its development. During his difficult ordeal, he much appreciated letters of encouragement from Bobby Knight and Dick Vitale and a phone call from Tom Izzo.

We also want to remember our parents—Tom and Elaine Staudt, and the late Fred and Alma Stabley—to whom we owe so much. We both feel blessed for their love, guidance, and wisdom.

Tim has drawn great support from his wife, Cathy, and they're proud of their three boys, Thomas, Matthew, and Patrick.

My No. 1 fan and best friend is my wife of nearly 36 years, Barbara. We thank God daily for our family: daughter Amy, husband Steve (Hirschman) and granddaughters Kaylee and Kaye; daughter Bethanie, husband Mark (Lambie) and granddaughter Karlie and grandson Kiplan; and son Kyle and his fiancée Stacy Zbikowski.

Contents

Acknowledgments

Tim and I appreciate all of the people who spent time with us reliving the championship years of the late 1970s. Without their assistance, we simply wouldn't have had a book.

Michigan State should feel fortunate to have had Jud Heathcote and Tom Izzo in charge of its basketball fortunes since 1976, moving the Spartans from the ranks of also-rans to a nationally elite program. Without their help and support, this would have been a much tougher project.

Most of the pictures used in the book came from the sports information office at Michigan State, and from super-fan Duane Vernon. Many thanks also to John Lewandowski and Paulette Martis from the SID office for their help.

Tim and I are certainly not members of the computer generation. We were kind of fond of our old manual typewriters. Fortunately, his son, Tom, and my son, Kyle, are computer literate. Their help was invaluable.

I looked to anyone who would critically read my contributions to this book, and I had plenty of volunteers in my daughter, Amy, and her husband, Steve Hirschman; my son, Kyle; my wife, Barbara; and my associate in the sports information office at Central Michigan University, a real basketball guru, Don Helinski.

Finally, we want to thank an old friend, Mike Pearson, who sought us out and entrusted us with the enjoyable task of writing *Tales of the Magical Spartans*. His guidance and foresight in this project helped us immensely.

Foreword

By Dick Enberg

It doesn't seem possible that 25 years have passed since the Michigan State Spartans used their special brand of magic to rule college basketball.

How times have changed since 1979! A peanut farmer from Georgia was our President ... "spam" was a type of canned meat, not an unwanted e-mail message ... and there were only 40 teams in the NCAA basketball tournament.

It was a time when players by the name of Bird, Greenwood, Moncrief, Tripucka, and Gminski thrilled college basketball fans with their special skills.

In 1979 at Michigan State University, Coach Jud Heathcote's Spartans played their home games in a venerable, drafty field house, not an air-conditioned modern arena.

I fondly remember my first visits to Jenison as a high school student from Armada, Michigan. My friends and I would hitch-hike over to East Lansing for the state high school championships. To these small village farm boys, Jenison was enormous; we couldn't believe a basketball place that big existed. The excitement and anticipation that was generated in the state finals will forever be etched in my mind. And while the arenas of today might have more comfortable seats and better sightlines, nothing can match the unique "field house" charm that was Jenison Field House.

And what excitement there was in 1978-79! The first Spartans game that Al McGuire, Billy Packer, and I covered for NBC television that season was against Kansas on a Sunday afternoon in February. At the time, MSU wasn't playing well, having struggled against an undermanned Northwestern team the day before. Jud was worried that his team wouldn't even finish among the top three in the Big Ten. But on that Sunday, before a national television audience, Michigan State completely dismantled the Jayhawks. I think that was the performance that ultimately catapulted the Spartans to a national championship.

Another game that I remember vividly was the Spartans' NCAA tournament showdown against Notre Dame in the regional finals in Indianapolis. Digger Phelps had a superb team, talent-wise, probably better than his Final Four club of 1977. I was of the opinion that whichever team won that game would be the national champion, and my prediction came true. From Mike Brkovich's dunk after the opening tip, all the way to the final buzzer, Michigan State was absolutely super.

Then came the semifinal game against Pennsylvania. I remember looking at the scoreboard with about 10 minutes to go in the first half. Penn had called another timeout. It was something like 40 to 8 in favor of Michigan State. I looked at Al and Billy and said, "I can't believe this is only the first half. We've got a whole second half to go, and this is a disaster." I still kid about that game being our longest hour, recognizing it was over shortly after it started.

And, then, of course, who can ever forget the title game between the Spartans and the Sycamores of Indiana State. There was a tremendous national media buzz that built to the opening tip, and basketball fans tuned into NBC-TV in record numbers. There's no question about who was the better team. Indiana State had Larry Bird and a nice group of complementary players. But they weren't about to beat the tremendous one-two punch of Earvin Johnson and Gregory Kelser. It's much like having two great power hitters in the middle of the lineup. You can pitch around one, but it's really tough to deny both. The media already knew about Earvin, but the NCAA tournament proved to be Kelser's opportunity to showcase how truly valuable a player he was. I remember the remarkable manner of these two young men. With poise and uncommon maturity, they conducted themselves selflessly, all the while exhibiting such open joy at this season and game to remember. You had to be abnormal not to love Magic Johnson and Gregory Kelser.

A truly "magical" year for Michigan State's 1979 NCAA championship basketball team culminated with a hero's salute in a parade through the heart of Lansing. *Photo courtesy of MSU Sports Information.*

I have often been asked, "Will there ever be another Magic Johnson?" Well, what Earvin did for the game, for his teammates, for the University, and for the entire world of college basketball was absolutely unique. His smile would brighten the entire gymnasium and his high-octane play reflected that great enthusiasm of the boyishness within the man. Earvin's passes excited me far more than any spectacular shot, for the pass reflects the anticipation and the spirit of teamwork. I hope that he isn't one of a kind, but, I must admit, I haven't seen another player like him over the past 25 years. Earvin **was** Magic!

I'd like to think that I speak for the average fan, because that's all I have ever been in trying to appreciate greatness. Thank you, Spartans, for providing an incredible year full of the richest of "Oh, mys!"

Introduction

"The Quakers had also been to the Final Four, in 1979, with a center who was a concert pianist. Their players also spoke in complete sentences, and graduated..."

The Last Amateurs by John Feinstein

And whose players couldn't speak in complete sentences and didn't graduate?

Certainly not the members of Michigan State's 1979 NCAA championship team who not only spoke eloquently, and in complete sentences, but they graduated, too.

The icing on the cake was that they also could play basketball better than anybody in the college ranks, including the Pennsylvania Quakers from the Ivy League, whom the Spartans spanked 101-67 in the semis and left them, quite possibly, speechless.

One thing that I discovered in doing research for *Tales of the Magical Spartans* was how successful the members of that 1978-79 basketball team have become in life.

When their college days were over, 11 of the 13 graduated, and all of them took off on separate but successful paths. Don't feel sorry for the two who didn't get their diplomas, because Earvin Johnson and Jay Vincent have done quite well in the NBA and subsequent business dealings.

I was the Michigan State beat writer at *The State Journal* in Lansing during the championship season, and my co-author, Tim Staudt, was well on his way to becoming one of the storied media figures in Lansing history as a TV sports director at WJIM-TV.

Tales of the Magical Spartans is not the first time we collaborated on writing projects. I was the sports editor of the *East Lansing Towne Courier* in the mid-1960s, and my ace reporter was Tim Staudt.

The roles reversed later on when I worked for Tim, ever the entrepreneur, on a couple of his projects like the game program for the Michigan High School Athletic Association boys' basketball tourney and a detailed preseason magazine on high school football in Michigan. Tim has been one of my best friends for nearly 40 years. He's the godfather to my son, Kyle, and I'm the godfather to his son, Matthew. We've spent many, many hours on the golf course together.

An old Spartan friend, former assistant SID Mike Pearson, approached me about doing this book in the fall of 2001. I loved the idea but didn't want to do it alone. I had been gone from the Lansing area since 1982 when I moved to Mount Pleasant as the sports information director at Central Michigan University (the same job my father had at Michigan State from 1948-80).

While I had left the area, Tim had remained close to Michigan State, and I suggested to Mike that we get him to join as a co-author. We met at Tim's beautiful Okemos home in November of 2001 and discussed the possibility of a book.

Tim was a tad hesitant at first, but agreed and then became enthused as he jumped into the project. Our goal was to look back on that splendid era of MSU basketball and visit with all of the members of the Spartan family and those associated with the championship season. We wanted to pick their brains for memories, for untold stories, and for the highs and lows of that magical season.

Because I worked so closely with the "travel party"—those individuals who were at the practices and on the road trips—that was my charge. I was to run down all of those people, invade their memory banks, and find out what they've done in the past 25 years.

Tim knows everybody in Lansing, and he has great contacts with national figures like Dick Vitale, Digger Phelps, etc. He visited with those people and got their impressions of the 1978-79 Spartans.

For me, it was a glorious trip down memory lane. It was a chance to relive some of the most enjoyable moments of my life.

I was ambitious from the outset. I was determined to meet with all 13 players who cut down the nets in Salt Lake City on March 26, 1979 after defeating Indiana State in the finals, 75-64.

I met with Mike Brkovich during the 2001 holidays in his native Windsor, Ontario where he has gone back to make his fortune. We drove around Walkerville, half of which he seems to own, and had lunch at a little restaurant nearby.

He showed me his antique car collection, along with his office buildings, apartment buildings, and warehouses. Success has not spoiled Brkovich, who still called me "Mr. Stabley." He remains one of the most humble and polite people I've ever come across.

Next up was Ron Charles. We met at a Home Depot south of Atlanta when I was heading to Florida in the March of 2002. We held court for two hours at a nearby McDonald's, where he told me stories about working in the federal prison there. Physically, Bobo may have changed as much as any of them. The once reed-thin Charles weighed a sturdy 245 pounds, but he hadn't lost that soothing accent from his days in the Virgin Islands.

Terry Donnelly came back to Michigan State for a golf outing in May, and we chatted while he had breakfast at the Marriott in downtown East Lansing. Terry had not changed much and looked as though he could still hit that jumper from the baseline.

My wife, Barb, and I spent a delightful June afternoon at Gregory Kelser's new home in Franklin Hills. Gregory and his wife, Donna, were cordial hosts. With jazz, one of Gregory's passions, playing in the background, we spent much of the afternoon visiting.

Jay Vincent was a little harder to track down. He spends the majority of his time in Charlotte, N.C., although he still has business ventures in the Lansing area and gets back as often as possible. We got together at Bennigan's in Okemos. I kidded him about being "fashionably 10 minutes late," and he got back at me by spilling his Coke on me while flailing his arms to make a point. When Jay got out of his black Mercedes without one curl of hair on his head, he was a dead ringer for Shaquille O'Neal. He was insightful, honest and friendly, just like the Jay I knew so many years ago.

Two of the other players I had the fortune of getting together with in person were Donnie Brkovich, on a trip to Las Vegas, and Rick Kaye in Auburn Hills, near his DaimlerChrysler office.

One of the last interviews was a memorable one with the Magic man at Starbucks in East Lansing, a coffee café that Earvin owns.

Tim and I were convinced that scheduling a visit with the President of the United States or getting an audience with the Pope might have been easier than corralling Earvin. We'd been trying for a couple of months before our December 23 get-together.

We visited with Earvin early in November when the Magic Johnson All-Stars gave Tom Izzo's 2002-03 Spartans a hoops lesson in Breslin Arena. He was pressed for time but said he'd be back for six days at Christmas, and we could meet then.

A half a dozen phone calls after the Johnson family had flown in from California for Christmas resulted in nothing. Tim spent the Sunday afternoon before Christmas hanging around Breslin after learning that Earvin was going to be playing basketball there.

Finally, Earvin strolled in and Tim got it set up for the following afternoon.

It was well worth the wait. Earvin was glib, funny, and revealing.

Twice he got out of his chair in the back of Starbucks to imitate Jud Heathcote. He had us in stitches.

Through it all, Earvin's love, respect, and admiration for the old coach was clearly evident, as was his love of Michigan State and all of the mid-Michigan area. Despite his enormous success, he's never forgotten his roots and those who helped him along the way.

The rest of the interviews came on the phone, with the exceptions of Rob Gonzalez, a manager, Randy Bishop, and former assistant sports information director, Nick Vista, which were all done by e-mail.

Jud Heathcote comes back to East Lansing quite often, and Tim and I spent a couple of hours on a Sunday morning in a back room at Coral Gables. He was candid and friendly.

The one common thread I found in talking to all of the players was that they felt fortunate to have played at Michigan State for Jud. He could be irascible and cantankerous. But the man was principled and he could coach.

It hasn't been all peaches and cream for the Spartan family, though.

Rick Berry, son of MSU assistant coach, Bill, died at a very young age, shortly after making the NBA with the Sacramento Kings. He was the Spartans' ball boy in 1978-79.

Another assistant coach, Fred Paulsen, had to face a similar tragedy when his son Derek was killed the summer before his senior year in high school in an automobile accident. He was a 6'4" guard who was being recruited nationally (including Michigan State) despite playing in tiny Custer, S.D. His story was chronicled in *Sports Illustrated*.

Dave Harshman, an assistant coach, and Jay Vincent lost brothers, and Earvin's sister passed away, as did Belloli's wife Marie and manager Darwin Payton's first wife, Peggy.

All in all, however, *Tales of the Magical Spartans* is an upbeat look back at that glory season of 1978-79, a year that helped change basketball at Michigan State and college basketball, as a whole, forever.

We can only hope you enjoy reading it as much as we have enjoyed working on it.

—Fred Stabley Jr.

The Stabley name is special in the Staudt household and has been for years. We covered the same team together for the local newspaper, television and radio stations. But we'd known each other long before that.

Thank God Fred is a couple of years older than I am. Entering Michigan State, I wanted to do what his dad did—become a college sports information director. Fred Senior was considered among the best in the nation—the MSU football press box is named after his years of service, 1948-80. And he hired me on as a student my freshman year of college, 1967-68. We had one other student assistant in the office, two secretaries and Fred's able assistant, Nick Vista, who later became head SID when Fred Senior finally retired. Senior taught me plenty in my one year aboard and, frankly, so did Nick.

Then a part-time radio job became available and my goals changed.

Fred Junior and I attended East Lansing High School together and enrolled in one journalism class together. Junior is a superb amateur golfer and we've shared plenty of fun together on the course over the years. He is also a very able teacher, though I don't think he wants it known that I credit him for whatever prowess in the game I have today.

I am godfather to his son Kyle. I delivered the eulogy at Fred Senior's funeral in 1996, and over 32 years that's the only such eulogy I had ever been asked to deliver until I had the equally sad duty of talking about my brother at his funeral back on March 14, 2003.

Fred Junior was always a better church basketball player than I was, too—but then, he was taller.

He left the *Lansing State Journal* to write a specialty magazine on MSU sports, called *Spartacade*. It was very well done, but in a competitive market its life span was somewhat short. And I was happy to recommend to football coach Herb Deromedi that Central Michigan University would be fortunate to land a Stabley as its own sports information director. Fred got the job on his own talent, but I was happy to add icing to the cake.

So, having said all this, we were both pleased and excited when we were asked to co-author this book. We never fought once over who should write what. It was a labor of love for both of us, just like it is to spend free time together on the golf course with other friends.

We both were invited to Earvin's home in Los Angeles on separate occasions—Fred even played in his golf tournament once—I was invited and couldn't make it. We both owe a lot to all of the Magical Spartans for so many great memories that dominated a special two years in our lives.

—*Tim Staudt*

CHAPTER 1

Assembling
the Team

What an Era!

When the 1978-79 Spartans took to the court against Central Michigan to begin their magical season, I had been anchoring the sports for WJIM-TV for seven and one-half years. I was 29 years old at the time, and for three years I saw this coming. I had watched, along with Fred Stabley, Jr., of the *Lansing State Journal*, the development of Earvin Johnson at Lansing's Everett High School.

We both knew that this was a special player far beyond most high school players. As Fred's nicknaming of Earvin implied, he truly was a magical player. And some college was going to hit the jackpot in landing his signature to a scholarship.

Michigan State basketball struggled during Earvin's years in high school. Gus Ganakas was released after the 1976 season, and even though he did not leave a losing program for Jud Heathcote, interest in the community was mild. The games in Jenison Fieldhouse did not attract large crowds, nor did they for Jud's first year, either. But there was a built-up demand looming if Earvin Johnson would choose to stay home and become a Spartan.

Jud masterfully landed Earvin's buddy from Eastern High School, Jay Vincent, early in the recruiting season. Earvin and Jay had often talked of playing together after battling each other as high school rivals. The MSU coaches convinced Jay that by committing early he would establish his own stage, whether Earvin joined him or not.

The two were terrific team players and, of course, Jay went on to enjoy a distinguished NBA career in his own right. Holdover Greg Kelser offered some solid experience before he made an NBA name for himself. So those three, along with the other role players Jud put on the court with them, provided a terrific chemistry.

I'm convinced the Spartans were good enough to at least make the Final Four in Earvin's freshman year. MSU finished 25-5 and barely lost to Kentucky, 52-49, in a sloppy game at Dayton in the NCAA Regionals in March, 1978. The experience of that tournament paid dividends the next year. All of the young Spartans knew what to expect, just as Tom Izzo's players did in 2000 after making the Final Four in 1999.

Over the years, the question has often been debated—which MSU national championship team was better, 1979 or 2000? We'll never know because they were so different. The '79 team relied on essentially a six-man rotation, while the 2000 Spartans went nine to ten deep. Both teams had superb leadership, but Earvin ran the '79 team, and several seniors shared the load for Izzo. For what it's worth, in their prime, it's hard for me to believe Earvin's team would have lost in such a mythical matchup, simply because of his own greatness—but a case could easily be made for either one.

The MSU basketball bandwagon exploded on that April morning in 1977 when Earvin announced for Michigan State. All of the available tickets were immediately sold, and attending the games provided the ticket holders with a sense of local social prominence. Even though Jenison wasn't glittering like some of today's modern arenas, the basketball atmosphere was absolutely electric. There was no cable coverage in those days, and a local television basketball package was easily assembled because of the demand in the community to see the games.

I am convinced that these Spartans did a great deal for the university besides just win basketball games. Michigan State was coming off a lengthy football probation, and there was transition in the president's office after 28 years of strong leadership from John Hannah that ended with his retirement in 1969. The entire MSU community seemed to find a new sense of pride from the national acclaim the '78 and '79 Spartans received. And the fact that their best player was a home-grown product made it all just that much better. Earvin Johnson wasn't just a Michigan Stater—he was from Lansing, Michigan, which he, of course, told the world about throughout his NBA career whenever he was interviewed.

That I got to cover it all was special. I can't believe it has been 25 years. The memories remain vivid, and I doubt they will ever fade. I doubt we will ever see this kind of team assembled, at least at Michigan State, ever again. One worldly superstar, one head coach with enormous presence, some terrific players in the starting lineup paired up with some everyday Joes who knew their roles and contributed in special ways virtually every game. They were truly the Magical Spartans!

—*Tim Staudt*

A Memorable Phone Call

It was sometime in the summer of 1970. The telephone rang in the home of Paul Cook on Marshall Street in Lansing.

"Hello, Coach Cook ... my name is Earvin Johnson. I'm 11 years old and I want to know how I can attend your basketball camp."

With that phone call, the legend of one Earvin Johnson began to grow—several years before he would become Magic Johnson at Everett High School.

After two workouts at the Paul Cook Basketball Camp at what was then Gabriels High School in Lansing, the legendary coach went home and told his wife he had a special kid on his hands.

Paul Cook coached boys' and girls' high school teams in Jackson and Lansing for 51 years. He sent Jay Vincent to Michigan State from Lansing's Eastern High School.

"He was dominant against the older kids," Cook recalls. "I told Mary [his wife], I just hope he lives on the east side."

Gabriels High School is now Lansing Catholic Central, a mere 300 yards from the Cook home.

"One day when he was a senior at Everett High School, I saw Earvin downtown," Cook adds. "He was wearing his T-shirt from our basketball camp. It was tattered and didn't fit him any more, but he was still wearing it, and I never forgot that moment."

Earvin and Tucker

Earvin Johnson was a ninth grader at Lansing's Dwight Rich Junior High when he first met Charles Tucker.

The former Western Michigan University basketball player was leading a group counseling program that Earvin attended.

"The group was talking about life in general when the topic turned to basketball," Tucker recalled. "A couple of them started woofing a bit, and I told them that none of them could beat me."

Tucker took the more-than-eager youngsters to the gym and proceeded to "wipe them out."

From that point on, Earvin and Tucker became virtually inseparable.

"We played a lot of basketball, and we always battled," Tucker said. "Earvin didn't like the physical way I played against him, but he kept on coming back.

"He wanted to win, and that was right down my line. He wanted to learn, and I was there to help him."

Tucker taught Earvin at a young age how to win the NBA way.

"When the game is on the line, it's not a jumper but a layup and a foul," Tucker said.

It didn't take Tucker long to become convinced his young prodigy was going to be something special.

"He was such a competitor, and he cared about winning from the beginning," Tucker said. "Most young players are just interested in their own game."

Tucker credits this drive to succeed for developing Johnson's tremendous passing skills.

"Earvin always got the ball to the open man because he was trying to win," Tucker said. "The defenses would naturally concentrate on him, and he was more than happy to pass for an easy basket.

"He played with a lot of older guys and watched a lot of basketball on television with his father [Earvin Sr.]. He became a student of the game, a person who created passes."

In addition to endless "wars" on the court, Tucker took Earvin to many NBA games in Detroit and Indianapolis. Throughout it all, Tucker made sure that Earvin's parents knew exactly where he was and where he was going. He didn't want to usurp any of the parents' authority.

Tucker and Earvin Sr. became good friends and still are today. They get together at least once a week and attend church regularly on Sundays.

"Mr. Johnson is a solid guy," Tucker said. "He has good insight on people and sports, but because he's so quiet a lot of people don't know that. When it came to where Earvin was going to college, I knew he would turn to his father more than anyone else."

Fortunately for Michigan State, Earvin Sr. liked the Spartans and would point out reasons why his son would look good in green and white.

"I think I knew before young Earvin did that he was going to go to Michigan State," Tucker laughed. "He kept going back and forth between Michigan and Michigan State, but I knew his father would play a big role in the final decision."

Nearly 30 years later, Tucker and Earvin have remained good friends and still love to get together on the hardwood for a good "run" whenever Magic is back in Lansing.

While Tucker figured Earvin was going to be awfully good, nobody could have envisioned that he would help the Los Angeles Lakers to five NBA titles and be considered one of the best players ever to lace on a pair of sneakers.

"In my mind, he's one of the best four ever to play the game," Tucker said.

"I'd put him right there with Oscar Robertson, Michael Jordan, and Larry Bird."

Enough said!

When Earvin Became Magic

I was a 27-year-old sportswriter for *The State Journal* in Lansing when I first saw Earvin Johnson play basketball.

It was December of 1974, and I was assigned to cover Lansing Everett's season-opening tilt at nearby Holt High.

There had been rumblings for the past couple of years about this sensational young talent at Dwight Rich Junior High. He had set a city record by scoring 48 points in a game with four six-minute quarters. So I went to the game with great expectations.

The more veteran Holt team took Everett into overtime before the visiting Vikings prevailed, 50-49. Johnson, however, fouled out with 12 points and 10 rebounds.

I went back to the office, and everyone wanted to know about this Johnson kid. I told them that I felt he'd be a good player one day but he wasn't there quite yet. After all, he was only a sophomore.

As luck would have it, I was assigned Everett's next game. It was a home encounter with South Central Conference preseason favorite, Jackson Parkside.

Well, I was treated to a performance that night. Everett won by more than 30 points, and Earvin had 36 points, 18 rebounds, 16 assists and 10 steals.

It's not true that Earvin Johnson could leap tall buildings in a single bound while playing basketball at Lansing Everett High ... it just seemed that way. *Photo courtesy of Brian Burd, Lansing State Journal*

Of all the prep stars I'd watched through the years in Michigan—Chet Walker, Dave DeBusschere, Spencer Haywood and Campy Russell—I'd never seen anything like this.

I made my way to the basement locker room at Everett and sought out the young phenom. He was surrounded by a group of admiring young followers—his own entourage at 15 years old—when I got there.

I introduced myself when they left and said: "Earvin, we have to call you something. The Big E is out because of Elvin Hayes, and Dr. J is out because of Julius Erving. How about Magic?"

He looked at me with a twinkle in his eyes and said, "That's okay with me, Mr. Stabley."

And, that's how Earvin Johnson became "Magic."

—*Fred Stabley Jr.*

What a Promise!

Michigan State assistant coach Vern Payne didn't promise Gregory Kelser much to become a Spartan … just a national championship!

"I promise you'll win a national championship before you leave Michigan State," Payne said. "We're going to get Stuart House next year, and then we're going to get a kid from Lansing the following year [Earvin Johnson]."

While House ended up going to Washington State, MSU got two youngsters out of Lansing—Jay Vincent and Johnson.

"Jay turned out to be much better than House anyway," Kelser said. "It's kind of hard to believe how Vern's promise became reality."

To show you what kind of recruiter Payne was, Kelser never visited Michigan State until AFTER he signed his national letter of intent.

"Vern was a classy, engaging and honest person, and my parents loved him," Kelser said. "My father especially enjoyed his company."

Kelser finally visited East Lansing with his parents and brother Ray, and liked what he saw.

"It's a good thing, because it was too late then," Kelser laughed.

His first visit as a prep senior was to Minnesota, and he was high on the Gophers until an NCAA investigator showed up at his house following the trip. "He stayed for two hours," Kelser recalled. "He asked me a lot of questions, but Minnesota didn't offer me anything illegal."

Michigan State never entered the recruiting picture until Payne showed up at a Christmas tourney at Detroit Northwestern to watch Alan Hardy. Kelser outplayed him and went right to the top of the Spartans' wish list.

"Vern told me that we want you and you can play for us, and that sold me," Kelser said.

It Was Supposed to be a Package Deal

Gregory Kelser and Alan Hardy were roommates at a high school basketball tournament in Pennsylvania, and Michigan State assistant coach Vern Payne was in hot pursuit of both athletes.

He came to their room one night, suggesting that they both wear green and white.

"We talked about it that night and decided we'd sign the Big Ten letter of intent the following Monday," Kelser recalled. "He came to me first, and I signed. However, when he went to Alan's house, he said he couldn't sign.

"I felt betrayed, and it took me a long time to get over it. He said something about having a chance to visit Bob Knight at Indiana."

Hardy ended up at Michigan, where he sat on the bench for the first two seasons while Kelser became an All-American at Michigan State, won two Big Ten titles and an NCAA championship.

"It didn't bother me much when we played Michigan, and Hardy was on the bench," Kelser said. "Alan apologized when we were both in the Detroit Pistons' training camp following college, and we're friends now."

Coke and a Signature

When Vern Payne pulled up to Gregory Kelser's house in the spring of 1975, already waiting inside were representatives from Arizona State, Central Michigan and Detroit.

It was signing day, and all had full scholarships in hand for the slender forward from Detroit's Henry Ford High.

They were waiting for Kelser to come home from work at a nearby Hardee's.

Payne never got out of the car. Instead, he headed to Hardee's where Kelser was working behind the counter.

"I'll have a Coke and a signature," Payne said.

The startled Kelser obliged on both accounts. (He didn't charge Payne for the Coke.)

Quite a Phone Call!

It was a Wednesday night in the spring of 1977, and Gregory Kelser was busy studying in his dorm room when the phone rang.

It was a call that would change his life for the better.

"How would you like to play with Earvin 'Magic' Johnson?" queried Vern Payne, who had just taken the head job at Wayne State. "Well, you're going to get a chance to, because he's going to sign tomorrow morning."

Kelser, who had just finished a tough season under first-year head coach Jud Heathcote, was flying high.

"From that moment on, Jud could do what he wanted because now we were going to win," Kelser said.

And win they did.

MSU was 25-5 and Big Ten champs in 1977-78 and then won the NCAA title in 1978-79 after going 26-6 and tying for the conference crown.

Kelser recalled watching Earvin play in high school.

"When I got to Michigan State, all I heard about was this kid at Lansing Everett," Kelser said. "When I saw him play, I saw some tremendous passes and a wonderful setup guy. I envisioned myself on the end of those passes.

"You know what else I saw? Wherever Earvin went, people followed. He was like the Pied Piper."

He led them to Jenison Field House, where a ticket to a Spartan home game during Johnson's two-year stay was virtually impossible to come by. MSU registered 24 straight sellout crowds of 10,004.

Gus Urged Kelser to Stay

Gregory Kelser was confused and ready to find a new school after Michigan State had relieved Gus Ganakas of his coaching duties following the 1975-76 season.

If it weren't for Ganakas, and the fact that the Spartans had retained assistant coach Vern Payne, Gregory might have become "Special K" elsewhere.

"It really shook me up when Gus was fired," Kelser said. "I didn't like the idea of having to sit out a year, but I had had a solid freshman season and could have gone anywhere."

Kelser was pondering his future when he met with Ganakas in his office at Jenison Field House.

"Gus said that regardless of who comes to Michigan State, I should continue in the same direction," Kelser recalled.

"You belong here," Ganakas said.

"Now that struck me as being a bit unusual," Kelser said. "He was just fired but wasn't bitter toward Michigan State."

Kelser was fond of Ganakas and enjoyed his freshman season immensely.

"Gus was a good coach, very knowledgeable," Kelser said. "He was magnificent for me personally. He told me that I would start at the bottom and had to work my way up. I became a starter after the fourth game.

"Gus was the opposite of Jud Heathcote. Gus would point out positives and pat you on the back. Jud wouldn't."

The interesting fact about Ganakas's firing was that his last five teams were all winners, posting records of 13-11, 13-11, 13-11, 17-9 and 14-13. His seven-year career mark was 89-84.

Ganakas's most successful season, 1974-75, also proved to be the start of the end when MSU's black players staged a walkout before the Indiana game—a game the Spartans subsequently lost, 107-55, mostly with players off the junior varsity team.

Jud's Persistence Pays Off

Ron Charles wanted to play college basketball at St. John's University.

He was born and raised in Brooklyn before his folks moved to the Virgin Islands when Ron was 11. He wanted to go back to the big city, but his father, Leroy, was afraid he might get in with the wrong crowd.

One place he did not want to go was Montana, but its coach (Jud Heathcote) wouldn't take no for an answer.

"Jud had seen me play in the Pan Am Games," Charles said. "He started calling, but there was no way I was going to Montana.

"I can remember being called to the office a couple of times in high school, and I never got in trouble, so I knew it must be Jud calling again. He just kept on calling and I kept on saying 'no.'"

Charles refused to take a visit to Montana, but when Heathcote got the Michigan State job in the spring of 1976, he agreed to check out East Lansing.

The gods must have been looking after the Spartans that weekend.

"It was 65 degrees out and everyone was wearing shorts," Charles recalled. "I hit it off great with Gregory Kelser and Bob Chapman, and Coach Payne, too."

Charles signed with the Spartans, but after spending seven years in the Virgin Islands, the Michigan winters were always a challenge for the slender 6'8" forward.

"I never did get used to it," Charles said, with a chuckle. "I dealt with it, and it seemed to get better as the years went by."

Ron went home over the Christmas break in his freshman season and his teammates were betting he'd never return. He nearly didn't.

"I got on the airplane and I started crying," Charles said, about his return to the states. "I said to myself, 'What am I doing here?'"

It's a bit of an ironic twist that for the first six years after Charles's 1980 graduation from MSU he chose to live in ... Detroit.

Charles Was Looking to Leave

Ron Charles was prepared to leave Michigan State University after his sophomore season.

"If Vern Payne had gotten a bigger job than Wayne State, I might have followed him," Charles said. "Coach Payne told me to stay and that things were about to get better. I still wanted to go but not to Wayne State.

"Coach Payne knew what he was talking about. We signed Earvin Johnson and Jay Vincent, and we were on our way. Heck, I have no regrets about staying. We won an NCAA title."

Winning the NCAA championship never really struck Charles until many years later.

"We went out to Salt Lake City expecting to win," Charles said. "We felt we had even a better team the year before when we lost to Kentucky [the eventual NCAA winners in 1978] in the regionals in Dayton.

"The 1979 team didn't have the depth the 1978 team did, but we still didn't think anybody could beat us. As the years go by and I've gone to some more Final Fours as a spectator, it's become much more special.

"Plus, I love watching our championship game when it comes on ESPN Classic."

Jud Never Saw Donnelly Play

Terry Donnelly was convinced he was going to play college basketball at Washington State.

Despite a solid prep career in St. Louis, Missouri, the 6'2" guard was not heavily recruited by Division I teams. When he was named MVP of a couple of postseason tourneys, George Raveling at WSU started recruiting him.

"I even won a slam dunk contest with Raveling there, and when he went back home I was pretty sure he was going to offer me a scholarship," Donnelly recalled. "However, he ended up signing a local guard from Pullman."

Exit George Raveling … enter Jud Heathcote.

The new Michigan State basketball coach was scouring the country for players when he talked to Raveling

"Raveling told Jud about me," Donnelly said. "Jud called and I visited the next week, and he offered me a scholarship without ever watching me play basketball.

"I had a great visit. Dan Riewald, Kevin Vandenbussche and Edgar Wilson took me around, and I loved it."

So much for huge recruiting budgets and those touted scouting services.

Donnelly: It Was Like Winning the Lottery

Terry Donnelly's freshman season at Michigan State was memorable for little more than its mediocrity.

The Spartans were 10-17, and the 6'2", 159-pound guard averaged 7.9 points in 27 games.

"We had only three or four thousand fans at each game," Donnelly said. "I'd heard a lot about these two local high school kids, and they were going to play this big showdown game in Jenison Field House.

"I went to the game and it was unbelievable. The place was sold out and the people were going nuts. It was the first time I'd ever seen Earvin Johnson and Jay Vincent play."

Donnelly got a closer look at Earvin and Jay that summer during some open gym games in Jenison and loved what he saw.

"They could hold their own and they were playing against some pros," Donnelly said. "Earvin was just killing everybody and he hadn't even started playing college yet.

"Even then Earvin could get a pass through three or four guys when nobody in the world would have even tried.

"It was like I won the lottery. We were coming off a so-so freshman season and these two guys show up. I knew something special was going to happen."

It happened right away when the Spartans went 25-5 in 1977-78, losing in the regional finals to eventual NCAA winner Kentucky, 52-49. MSU then went 26-6 and won the national title the following year.

Donnelly kind of wished it had been reversed.

"The NCAA finals were in St. Louis in 1978," he said. "I always wanted to go to the University of Missouri, and it would have been nice to go back and show a few people that they'd made a mistake."

Donnelly still gets the last laugh, though, when ESPN Classic runs the old championship films each February and March.

"We were so focused on winning the title in 1979 that when the game was over it never really hit us," he said. "It wasn't until many years later when it sunk in, and now we can reminisce each year when they replay those games on ESPN."

Jud Who?

When Jud Heathcote was named Michigan State's new head basketball coach in the spring of 1976, Spartan fans everywhere hollered out, "Jud Who?"

MSU athletics director Joe Kearney had tapped a little-known coach from the University of Montana to replace the popular Gus Ganakas.

A lot of names for the job were bantered around, but none of the Spartan faithful had Heathcote on their list.

Always blessed with a dry, piercing wit, Heathcote wowed the media and fans alike with his honesty and humor.

"I'm from Montana where the men are men and the women are too," was one of Jud's opening lines at public appearances his first year at MSU.

Before Heathcote ever came to East Lansing, I had a chance to talk to him on the phone for a story for *The State Journal*. During the course of the interview, I asked him if he'd heard of Earvin Johnson, figuring the Lansing Everett recruit could be the key to getting his green and white career off on the right foot.

"Oh, sure," Heathcote said, and then proceeded on to something else.

Later, when he got off the phone, he told his assistant coaches in Montana to find out all they could about a kid named Earvin Johnson in Lansing.

As the beat writer for *The State Journal* in the mid-1970s, I spent a lot of time with Jud. He never hesitated to chew me out if he didn't like something I had written, but I grew to respect him and appreciate his coaching ability.

He was often criticized for being too demonstrative on the bench, drawing more than his share of technical fouls. "I've coached that way all of my life, and as sure as I'm fat and bald, I'm not going to change," he said.

The guy was a winner. He was honest. He made himself available to the media. What else could you ask for?

—*Fred Stabley Jr.*

Unlucky Coach

In July of 1974, former Michigan basketball guard Doug Herner was preparing for another season as head coach at Lansing Sexton High School. And he was excited. He was about to coach an incoming tenth grader named Earvin Johnson.

Herner was familiar with Johnson's potential. The youngster had spent summers working out at the school, and Herner had seen firsthand the brilliant prospect he was about to inherit. But in those days, integrated busing was all the rage in cities like Lansing. And before the month ended, Herner learned that Johnson instead would attend Everett, a predominantly white school at the time. The only person in Lansing more disappointed than Herner was Earvin Johnson himself.

"It was the best thing that could have happened to Earvin," Herner said without a trace of bitterness 25 years later. "He made George [Fox] a better coach and me a lesser coach."

For the next three years, Herner watched as two future Spartan stars drove his Sexton Big Reds batty. Sexton went 0-15 from 1974-77 playing against Eastern with Jay Vincent and Everett with Earvin Johnson.

"We tried everything to beat both of them," Herner recalled. "They were both gentlemen after we played the games and I liked them both a lot.

"I think Earvin had his career high and low against us his junior year. He had a good supporting cast on his teams.

"I knew they'd both be pretty good at Michigan State. I just wish Jud would have taken them after their sophomore years in high school."

In the 1976-77 season, Sexton finished with just five losses. All five were to Everett and Eastern.

"Those two set the standards for Lansing high school basketball for years to come," Herner added. "Their styles of passing and team play showed all of the young players around them how it should be done."

Herner was a busy coach the night Michigan State won the NCAA title in Salt Lake City. He was tending bar during a party in the basement of MSU fan Duane Vernon's home. Sexton football coach Gary Raff and *Lansing State Journal* sportswriter Bob Gross helped out serving spirits to jubilant MSU fans several hundred strong.

Herner coached at Sexton several more seasons before retiring. He kept his hand in the game by working MSU summer camps for Jud Heathcote. He has remained in that role and has added many additional duties for Tom Izzo's camps.

First Impressions

When was the first time Jud Heathcote saw Earvin Johnson play basketball?

It was in the MSU intramural gymnasium shortly after Earvin's junior year. He was involved in a pickup game that included former Spartan great Terry Furlow. Earvin looked up to Furlow, the two were friends, and Furlow always invited Earvin to play in the summer games.

Jud was impressed with the way Earvin took control of the games and Furlow did not.

Shortly after Jud started recruiting Earvin Johnson seriously, he and athletic director Joe Kearney were called in to see MSU president Clifton Wharton.

"I do not like the position you have put me in," Wharton told them. "I do not want to be involved in the pressure to recruit Earvin Johnson."

The meeting left Kearney a bit shaken. Jud put it out of his mind and continued his recruiting duties as usual.

Jud got off to a slow start with Earvin. He attended an Everett game where autographed basketballs were being sold by the school, and Earvin's signature, of course, was on them. Jud got one.

Earvin told him that night, "It's the only signature you'll ever get from me." He did get another one, but Jud never forgot the incident.

Jud and George

It didn't take long for George Fox and Jud Heathcote to become friends after the new Michigan State coach determined that Earvin Johnson would be a prime recruit.

"Jud was his own man," Fox recalls. "I told him all about Earvin's potential as a ball-handling guard for the Spartans. By Earvin's junior year, Jud knew 100 percent about Earvin's point guard potential. We talked about how Earvin could break the double team by throwing the ball over the top against the defense."

Back in the 1970s, most of the area high school coaches received complimentary tickets to MSU basketball home games, and Fox was more than eager to attend. He sat behind the MSU bench with his peers, and that's where George sits today in the Breslin Center, compliments of Tom Izzo.

After Earvin signed with the Spartans, Jud kept Fox in the loop about his former star and his role with the Spartans.

"I enjoyed every part of the whole MSU experience," Fox says. "Jud made me a big part of it."

The two coaches attended the McDonald's All-American high school all star game in Washington, D. C., just prior to Earvin's commitment.

"Earvin never told me where he was going to go to college," Fox recalls. "But I told Jud at the McDonald's game I was sure he was going to get him. He asked, 'How do you know?'

"I told him the kids around him convinced me he was going to Michigan State. Earvin was just never going to leave his friends. I was sure of it."

Jud Sold on Jay Early

There's no question that Jud Heathcote had a good eye for talent.

While recruiting was not his favorite part of being a head college basketball coach—"I'd rather worry about what I have than what I don't have," he'd often say—it didn't take him long to become a Jay Vincent fan.

The 6'8" 225-pounder from Lansing Eastern High was having a quietly brilliant career for the Quakers, albeit in the Paul Bunyan-like shadow of Lansing Everett rival Earvin Johnson.

"If it hadn't been for Earvin, Jay probably would be remembered as the greatest player Lansing's ever had," Heathcote said. "I liked Jay from the start. He had great hands, but we didn't have to beat the world for him."

While many schools throughout the Midwest recruited Vincent initially, hoping to land a Johnson-Vincent pact as they had often talked about, many eventually bowed out. That was just fine with Jud. He wanted Jay regardless.

Many recruiters felt Jay was too short to play center and too slow to play forward. Jud simply said, "Jay can play; it doesn't matter what position."

Shortly after bowing out of the Class A prep tournament in 1977, Vincent committed to the Spartans and then proceeded to have a wonderful four-year stay in East Lansing.

"Jay had been in Earvin's shadow for so long that we convinced him that if he signed with us before Earvin made his decision it would be special, and he did," Jud said. "However, Jay couldn't understand why he still couldn't take his recruiting trips. We told him not only was it unethical, but illegal."

Averaging 21.5 and 22.6 points per game in his junior and senior seasons, Vincent left Michigan State as the second-leading

Nobody got to see the "real" Jay Vincent in Michigan State's postseason run to the NCAA championship because of a foot injury sustained in the tourney opener against Lamar. *Photo courtesy MSU Sports Information*

scorer in Spartan annals with 1,814 points. Only Gregory Kelser was any better at the time with 2,014.

Entering the 2003-04 campaign, Vincent still stood fifth in MSU's all-time list behind Shawn Respert (2,531), Steve Smith (2,263), Scott Skiles (2,145) and Kelser.

Twice a first-team All-Big Ten selection and Big Ten Player of the Year in 1981, Vincent had his No. 31 retired on Jan. 9, 1999.

Recruiting Jay

Michigan State landed Jay Vincent well ahead of Earvin Johnson in the Spartans' 1977 recruiting class, but Jay's coach Paul Cook thinks Jay's verbal commitment had little impact on Earvin's eventual decision to become a Spartan.

"I really didn't get involved in Jay's recruitment," Cook says. "I always thought he would end up at Michigan State, but he was a quiet kid and I didn't visit with him very much about it. Earvin's decision was totally independent of Jay's, although they were friends off the floor. They were fierce rivals on the court, though."

After Jay became a Spartan, Jud Heathcote only consulted Cook on an informal basis about advice in coaching him.

"We never had any in-depth discussions," Cook recalls. "I knew Jay would become a very good player on a very good college team.

"I think Don Monson [MSU assistant coach] was a big factor in helping Jay succeed at State. Earvin was more resourceful in dealing with Jud and Jay was more sensitive when Jud would get on him. Monson was very good at taking Jay aside and talking with him and soothing things over when necessary."

Frustration!

Paul Cook's Lansing Eastern High School Quakers played Earvin Johnson's Everett Vikings eight times from 1974-

77, the three seasons of his high school career. Eastern won just one time, 70-62, late in the regular season of Earvin's senior year. The game was moved to MSU's Jenison Fieldhouse to handle the crush of fans, and the place was packed with 10,000 spectators.

In their first meeting of Earvin's senior year, Eastern had a 13-point lead over Everett in the inaugural game at Eastern's Don Johnson Fieldhouse. But by the end of regulation play, Earvin led his team back to tie the score, and the Vikings won in overtime behind Johnson's 44 points.

When Earvin and Jay Vincent last faced each other in high school, Everett won, 63-41, in the opening district game of the state tournament on the Quakers' floor. The game was televised live, the first such telecast of a high school game in the mid-Michigan area.

Eastern had lost its stellar guard, Victor Jackson, to a season-ending injury several games before, and the Quakers simply couldn't match up to beat Everett as they did several weeks earlier in Jenison.

For Three Pigs
in a Blanket ...

Gregory Kelser and Bob Chapman like to tell people that they recruited Jay Vincent for Michigan State with "three pigs in a blanket and two large milks."

The two were hosts for the 6'8" Lansing Eastern High standout on his official visit to MSU, and they took him to the International House of Pancakes for dinner.

"Jay went into IHOP saying that 'you guys' should be pretty good next year," Kelser said. "When he left, he was saying that 'we're' going to be good next year.

"I don't think Jay was going to leave Lansing anyway. He didn't like road trips. One of my biggest regrets was that he was hurt and didn't play much in our championship run, because he was so valuable all season long."

Announcement Day!

Earvin Johnson's college announcement day was the most notable sports day in the greater Lansing area that I can ever remember. Michigan State basketball had been down.

The Spartans were coming off a 10-17 season with a grumpy coach named Jud Heathcote in charge, and no one in town really knew whether this was the guy to change the team's fortunes around or not. But they all knew about Earvin "Magic" Johnson.

In those days there weren't as many media people around chasing the big recruiting story as there are today. It was pretty well figured that Earvin would choose Michigan or Michigan State–but it was a much tougher guess for everyone to pick which one of those two was going to get this prized player.

Earvin kids me to this day that I always said he would end up at Michigan. The truth is I thought he might end up there, but I never said so on the air—anywhere!

The night before his announcement, Jud attended a dinner at Walnut Hills Country Club in East Lansing where I was present, and I couldn't read his body language to figure where Earvin was headed or if Jud even knew himself.

Driving back to the office that night to prepare the 11 o'clock sports, I heard Johnny Orr, the Michigan coach, being interviewed on Detroit's WJR radio.

"We're keeping our fingers crossed for tomorrow," Orr said. "We think we've got a good shot. We've recruited him well." Orr sounded to me like he might know something.

The plan the next morning, a Friday, was for Earvin and his family to make the big announcement in the Everett High School auditorium. The microphones were piped around the entire school, but there was no live television or radio coverage. As soon as I got the word, I would call WJIM-TV and radio, and they could spread the message.

Earvin sat down and asked. "Are there any questions?"

After the laughter died down, he simply said, "Next year, I will be attending Michigan State University." With that I ran down the hall to a telephone, and Michigan State basketball was about to change forever.

Earvin had actually signed the papers with the university the previous day. And he had made up his mind on Wednesday after a visit from departing MSU assistant coach Vernon Payne.

Payne had recruited Earvin hard, but right after the Spartans' season ended, Payne landed the head coaching job at Wayne State University in Detroit. On that Wednesday, he had come across Michigan assistant coach Bill Frieder in an East Lansing restaurant, busy, of course, chasing Earvin Johnson for the Wolverines.

With that Payne headed for Everett High School and told George Fox he wanted to see Earvin right away. He told Earvin that he was leaving Michigan State, but that Jud Heathcote was the guy he still ought to play for in college.

To the surprise of most, Earvin agreed right there on playing for Michigan State, and Vern called Jud and told him to get the signing papers ready.

To this day, people say Earvin never would have played for Michigan, but I do not agree with that. Earvin would have signed with Michigan State in short order had Gus Ganakas remained as the Spartans' head coach. He and Gus had become friends early in his high school career.

Michigan knew there was an opening when Ganakas was let go and jumped on the opportunity. Plus, the Heathcote personality was in marked contrast to what Earvin had experienced with Gus.

I thought Michigan did a tremendous job on Earvin during his senior year. Earvin wore Michigan clothing and he liked the Michigan players and coaches. Those in the Lansing area say Earvin never would have left and disappointed all of the area fans. We'll never know, but I believe Vernon Payne's meeting two days before his actual announcement sealed the deal for

Michigan State. Vernon Payne may have been the real hero for the Spartans in the recruitment of Earvin "Magic" Johnson.

—*Tim Staudt*

Recruiting Earvin

"Y ou can print this—I'm glad I didn't go to Michigan." Earvin Johnson was reflecting back on his final recruiting decision to become a Spartan in the spring of 1977, and the Wolverines did come close to landing the Everett High School All-American.

"I wanted to attend Michigan State my whole life," Earvin said. "But I put Michigan in the lead in my mind after Gus Ganakas got fired.

"It was tough because I wanted to play for Gus. Understand I had gone to every Michigan State football and basketball game my whole life."

Soon after Jud Heathcote was named the Spartans' new head coach, Earvin was playing in a four-on-four pickup game in Jenison Field House's old upper gym. Earvin had played in many such games during his youth.

The assistant coaches on the MSU staff brought Jud to watch, and soon the Heathcote/Johnson relationship began.

"Vern Payne did most of the talking. As the season went along [Earvin's senior year at Everett], I got to know Jud better," Johnson said.

There weren't as many detailed recruiting rules in those days as there are today, and so visits from college coaches were frequent. That worked well for Michigan's dogged assistant, Bill Frieder, who did much of the legwork for the Wolverines' head man, Johnny Orr.

"Frieder was everywhere," Earvin said.

The night before Earvin's final announcement, Orr was a guest on Detroit radio station WJR. He said he was still hopeful of landing Johnson but that he hadn't heard one way or the other whether the winner would be the Spartans or the Wolverines.

Earvin went back and forth with both schools in his mind through the final weeks of March. He leaned on his father for advice as he has done his entire life.

"My dad said he would support me whatever I decided. He was hoping for Michigan State because he said he could see me play more," Earvin said.

But the final decision was made for the Spartans after an impromptu meeting between Earvin and Vern Payne. The MSU assistant had just been named head coach at Wayne State in Detroit. He told Earvin he had nothing to gain by recommending Michigan State at that point and he convinced Johnson that Jud Heathcote would make him a better player and prepare him for the NBA. The rest is history. And Earvin has never had second thoughts about his college choice.

During the recruiting process the students at Everett High School became excited when they heard Indiana's famed Bobby Knight would visit their school to see if Johnson might consider a visit to the Bloomington campus.

"It was a great moment when I met him," Earvin said. I found him so different than what I'd seen from his coaching personality. But we never met again after that one meeting—he couldn't believe I didn't want to make a visit, but I knew that I wasn't going to end up playing at Indiana."

From Homer to Everett

When Jaimie Huffman's prep coach retired from Homer High, the talented young hoopster decided to transfer for his senior season.

He had seen Earvin Johnson play basketball, and he dreamed of the opportunity of being on the same floor with the Lansing Everett superstar.

His older brother, Damon, was already in Lansing at the Cooley Law School, and the 6'3" Huffman moved in with him and enrolled at Lansing Everett.

"It was a privilege to play basketball at Michigan State on the national championship team," Huffman said. "But on a personal level, playing at Everett and winning the Class A state championship was my greatest sports moment.

"I was a key player and a contributor on the state championship team. It was quite a thrill to win it, and Earvin became a good friend. I loved playing for George Fox. He was a great coach who knew how to get the best out of everyone.

"I was so pumped after winning that I didn't sleep for two days."

Two years later, Huffman shared another great moment in Salt Lake City with Johnson when they cut down the net for an NCAA championship.

Not bad for a kid from Homer.

Best of Both Worlds

Ever the free spirit, Greg Lloyd made light of his return to Michigan State as a transfer from the University of Arizona.

"I wasn't playing at Arizona, so I figured I might as well go home and not play there," the former Lansing Eastern standout joked. "But you know, it worked out for the best. I got to play on a national championship team, and then I moved back to Tucson and made it my home."

Lloyd spent two years in Arizona after being recruited there by the "Desert Fox," Fred Snowden.

"I loved the area, but it didn't work out for me as a player," he said. "I still had family in Lansing and decided to move back."

Lloyd has a lot of fond memories of his two years with the Spartans—1977-78 and 1978-79. He redshirted the first season and then played in 19 games and scored 27 points in the championship campaign.

"The great thing about that team is that there were no cliques," Lloyd said. "We were a cohesive team that all hung out together.

Gregory Lloyd was a "free spirit" who often did or said the craziest things. He's now enjoying life with his wife and two children in Phoenix. *Photo courtesy of MSU Sports Information*

"It was a bunch of good guys who didn't do drugs, and drinking wasn't a major part of our lives. We were a close-knit group and that helped us through a lot of tough times."

One that Lloyd remembers clearly was the night the Spartans lost their No. 1 ranking in the nation at Illinois. MSU was 9-1 and the 14-0 Illini were fourth in the country.

An 18-foot jumper on the baseline by Eddie Johnson gave Illinois the 57-55 win.

"Gregory Kelser slipped trying to cover Johnson, he hits the jumper and 'boom,' just like that, our No. 1 ranking was gone," Lloyd said. "We got it back at the end when it really counted, though."

Name Your School

S ports quiz: what Michigan State basketball player on the 1979 team, next to Earvin Johnson, could have picked his college coming out of high school?

No, it wasn't Gregory Kelser. And it wasn't Jay Vincent.

It was none other than 6'7" Rob Gonzalez, a highly recruited player from Detroit Catholic Central who averaged 27 points and 13 rebounds a game as a prep senior.

The 207-pound forward selected the Spartans over Ohio State, Maryland, North Carolina, Michigan and Tennessee, to name a few.

"I chose Michigan State because of the team's potential and being able to play with Earvin," Gonzalez said. "Plus it was close to home.

"It was a great learning experience for me, and winning the national title made it special."

Gonzalez had to laugh when he read where Michigan head coach John Orr said that the only player in the state that he wanted and lost to Michigan State was Earvin Johnson.

"That struck me as kind of funny because he practically lived at my house at my senior year," Rob recalled. "And when I signed at MSU, he called me on the phone and was really mad."

Rob didn't finish his career in green and white, however.

He transferred to the University of Colorado after his sophomore season in East Lansing. "It worked out well for me on both accounts," Gonzalez said. "I enjoyed my stay at Michigan State, and I felt that maybe a change was necessary for me to grow as a human being as well as a player."

Gonzalez averaged 10.3 points a game and shot .523 from the field (114-218) as a junior and then sported a 9.5 mark as a senior when he hit an incredible 91.5 percent from the free throw line (75-of-82).

He started 50 of 55 games in his two years in Boulder, meshing a career high of 21 points at Kansas in 1983—the last time the Buffaloes won over the Jayhawks on the road.

No Recruiting Battle Here

J ud Heathcote won a huge recruiting battle when he signed
Earvin Johnson in the spring of 1977.

When he inked Mike Brkovich later that spring, he didn't
beat one school.

"Jud really went out on a limb to sign a kid from Windsor
[Ontario] who wasn't recruited by anybody," Brkovich said. "I'll
always be indebted to him for that. I had to be a big gamble for
him."

Brkovich grew up in hockey-happy Windsor, right across
the river from Detroit, but gravitated to basketball because he
was taller than most hockey players (6'4"). A YMCA was located
across the street from his house, and it had a good basketball
program.

He starred at Lowe High but was a front-line player because
of his size—another strike against him being a Division I prospect.
He'd have to play guard in college, and his ball-handling skills
were suspect.

But oh, how he could shoot.

Brkovich played a lot of pickup ball with some talented
players whose families had moved from Detroit. One was so
impressed with Mike's game that he started calling coaches in
Michigan.

Eastern Michigan's Ray Scott was interested after watching
him play but had no scholarships and wanted to place him at a
junior college. Heathcote saw him play a couple of times and
then offered him a scholarship.

"His high school coach [Gerry Brumpton] told me he could
play, but he didn't show me anything the first time I saw him,"
Heathcote remembered. "Gerry told me he was so nervous and
that he was a lot better than that. I saw him again and he was
much better."

Brkovich still shakes his head when thinking about coming
to MSU.

"It was pretty incredible," Brkovich said. "I'd never visited
Michigan State or saw a game live. And I didn't know much

about Earvin Johnson, Gregory Kelser, Jay Vincent or Jud Heathcote, for that matter."

About the only thing that Brkovich did know about Michigan State came from watching the Big Ten *Game of the Week* on TV.

"I watched Terry Furlow score 50 points against Iowa on TV, but that was about it," recalled Brkovich. "It was a great break for me to come to Michigan State."

For the Spartans, too.

Small Family in a Big Campus

Michigan State had an enrollment of more than 43,000 in the late 1970s, but it didn't seem that big to Mike Longaker because of his extended family in East Lansing—his Spartan basketball teammates.

"You spend so much time together that you really get close," Longaker said. "It was a neat experience when you take a group of different individuals and blend them together with one common goal of winning.

"Once we got Earvin Johnson and Jay Vincent in 1977, winning became a realistic goal."

More than the wins, Longaker remembers the road trips where it was Michigan State's traveling party of 20 against the opponents' 20,000.

"There was so much teasing and kidding on the team," Longaker recalled. "Most of it was good-natured ... some of it wasn't.

"Jud Heathcote had a tremendous sense of humor, although it was hard to appreciate it when it was directed at you."

Longaker remembers how impatient Heathcote would be at dinner.

"Jud would order his steak rare," Longaker said. "Because of that, he figured his should always be done first and he should be served first.

"More than once, Jud went out to the kitchen to find out where his steak was."

It was on road trips that Longaker, a physiology major with a 3.9 GPA, helped his teammates with their studies.

"We had a pretty bright group of guys, and it didn't take much to help them," said Longaker. "They'd usually come with a specific question. They were good students."

They may have been good students, but Earvin Johnson said the No. 1 question whenever we checked into a hotel on the road was "What's Aker's room number?"

"And you'd better get there early or there would be a line of guys in the hall," Earvin laughed. "He was always the most popular guy on the team when we were on the road."

Lansing Ties

Throughout the years, Earvin Johnson has always proclaimed with pride that he grew up in Lansing, Michigan and is proud of his roots. Through his various interviews and appearances on radio and television shows, Earvin has proudly told of his childhood memories from days in Lansing where he lived through his sophomore year at Michigan State.

"I am proud to have grown up in Lansing," Earvin said. "The people know me as Earvin. It's where I grew up. It will always be home for me. It's where I got my base and my values. I love to give back to the community when and however I can. I would never trade growing up here. People in Los Angeles are so different from those in Lansing. I think of people in Lansing as very hard-working people."

Several times a year, Earvin returns home to his mother and father, who live in an upscale home on Lansing's northwest side. Earvin's wife, Cookie, can visit her parents at the same time in the Detroit area.

Whenever Earvin returns, the routine is just about always the same. He works out at the Michigan Athletic Club and follows that with pickup games in the Breslin Center with close friends.

CHAPTER 2

The Formative Years

Let Me Top That

Gregory Kelser had an incredible Big Ten debut, scoring 10 points and collecting 23 rebounds in a 70-63 loss at Wisconsin in 1975-76.

The late Terry Furlow came up to the slender 6'8" freshman after the game and said, "That was unbelievable. I'll have to top that."

"It was nothing special to me because I had done that a number of times in high school," Kelser said. "But that turned out to be the only time I ever had 20 in my career."

As for Furlow, he scored 50 points against Iowa, 48 against Northwestern and 42 against Ohio State in his next three games.

Advantage Furlow!

That Jumper Won't Do

Jud Heathcote couldn't believe his eyes ... Terry Donnelly couldn't believe his ears.

It was the first week of school in 1976, and the left-handed shooting freshman guard from St. Louis, Mo., was playing in a four-on-four pickup game in courts upstairs at Jenison Field House.

The Spartan mentor happened by and watched a bit of the action.

Donnelly pulled up in front of Heathcote and buried a 20-footer from the corner.

"Stop," bellowed the stoop-shoulder coach. "What the hell was that?

"That was the worst-looking shot I ever saw. You will never play at this school with a shot like that."

The crestfallen Donnelly's spirits jumped, though, when Heathcote said, "I'll have to spend a lot of time with you in the gym."

And he did.

"We met an hour before practice each day," Donnelly recalled. "It took quite a while, but Jud knew a lot about shooting and was a great teacher."

So great, in fact, that Donnelly was a key factor in the NCAA championship win over Indiana State.

"It was the only time in my whole career that Jud told me to shoot," Donnelly said, laughing.

Donnelly responded by nailing all five shots from the floor and five of six free throws.

Bad Choice

There's nothing like getting off on the wrong foot. Just ask Rick Kaye.

Michigan State's 6'7" freshman from Detroit Catholic Central was all set to go to mandatory study hall in the fall of 1977 when his roommate convinced him otherwise.

"It's the first week; you don't have to go to study hall," said Terry Donnelly, a wise old sophomore. "Let's go out."

Although Kaye balked, Donnelly finally convinced him and the two went off for a fun evening on the town.

"Can you imagine a guy I looked up to using his sophomore influence to get me in trouble?" Kaye said with a twinkle in his eye. "When we got back to the dorms, the guy across the hall said that Jud Heathcote and Don Monson [assistant coach] were knocking on my door earlier looking for me. I knew I was in big trouble. Jud didn't speak to me for days."

Kaye and Donnelly have remained close friends, getting together at least once a year during the winter to reminisce and take in some Michigan State basketball games. No doubt they both have a good laugh over Rick missing his very first study hall.

A Freshman on the Cover?

Nick Vista spent 33 years in the sports information business, first as an assistant and then as the head SID at Michigan State University.

Only once in all those years did he ever remember a freshman on the cover of a Spartan media guide ... Earvin Johnson in 1977.

"I remember mentioning to Jud about using the statue of Sparty as a backdrop for the cover," Vista said. "He liked the idea and suggested using the co-captains [Bob Chapman and Gregory Kelser] along with his great freshman, Earvin Johnson.

"It must have been okay, because we used the same theme on the cover the next year with Gregory and Earvin."

Earvin "Magic" Johnson and Gregory Kelser grace the cover of Michigan State's 1978-79 media guide. They were also on the 1977-78 cover with Bob Chapman. *Photo courtesy of MSU Sports Information*

In Private Please

Nothing Gregory Kelser did in his early years with Jud Heathcote as the Michigan State head coach ever seemed to be good enough.

Kelser had a splendid freshman season, averaging 11.7 points and 9.5 rebounds per game (second best in the Big Ten), in his only year playing for Gus Ganakas.

Heathcote took over before the 1976-77 campaign, and the 6'8", 189-pound Kelser became the subject of constant verbal assaults.

"He told me that I couldn't play and that my shot was no good," Kelser recalled. "He used to just wear me out so much that I didn't enjoy going to practice. When you don't do anything right every single day, it's tough.

"My dad [Walter] was a military guy, and there was not a whole lot of sympathy coming from him. I figured out pretty early that the key was to listen to what he was saying, not how he was saying it.

"Jud was like a football coach, only he was coaching basketball."

The one thing that Kelser appreciated about Heathcote's style was that he didn't play mind games with playing time like Bob Knight did at Indiana.

"He would shout and berate you, but I knew I was going to start the next game and get a chance to improve," he said.

Kelser had had enough during a coaching clinic at Jenison Field House when Heathcote rode him in front of a packed house.

"It was embarrassing and humiliating," Kelser said. "I called for a special meeting with Jud and said that it was okay to be singled out in practice in front of my teammates but I never wanted to be publicly humiliated again.

"In his own way he acknowledged it, and never again did he take shots at me publicly."

Although a tad hesitant, Kelser agreed to work the coaches' clinic the following year, and Heathcote was as complimentary as he was negative the year before.

Dickie V...

In 1979, the basketball world did not know Dick Vitale the way he is known today. In that year, Vitale figured he was just about finished with the game and was discouraged with his lot in life, to say the least. He'd been fired as head coach of the Detroit Pistons after serving as head coach and later athletic director at the University of Detroit.

The ESPN network did not exist the year the Spartans won the national title—but it was on its way. The network was being formed, and one of the producers had heard Vitale give a speech several years earlier before his U-of-D Titans were about to play in an NCAA tournament game.

Vitale's enthusiasm as a speaker was noticed by others, and he was invited to try out as an analyst doing college games for ESPN. He almost did not accept the invitation but for the encouragement of his wife Lorraine. The rest, as they say, is history.

Today, Vitale is 63 years old and is arguably the most famous broadcast personality in college basketball. He has worked for ESPN ever since it went on the air, shortly after the Spartans won in Salt Lake City. And he well remembers the 1979 championship game in which the Spartans beat Indiana State.

"That game, pitting Magic vs. Bird, created the unbelievable feeling for the world of college basketball on television," Vitale says.

"It kicked off the unbelievable interest in March Madness. It set the tempo for the biggest growth in college basketball."

Vitale, like so many others, was a huge fan of what Earvin Johnson did for his Spartans and for the game in general.

"He was Mr. Versatility. He created the thought in other coaches that big guards could exist and distribute the ball," said Vitale. "His kind of talent laid the groundwork for other players who were tall and also multi-dimensional. Other big guards who have come along haven't been as talented as Magic, but they showed they could contribute big-time.

"Earvin was so good with his passing, and I loved his unbelievable unselfishness. He demonstrated that it is possible for a tall player to play three different positions well."

The 1979 NCAA championship game still holds the record for the highest television rating for a college basketball game of all time. That year, 48 teams were entered in the tournament. In 1983, the field expanded to 64, and while ESPN does not hold the contract to cover the games live, its seemingly endless coverage during March clearly has helped lead to the continued growing interest among fans around America. And, of course, Dickie V has been the biggest cheerleader for the NCAA tournament of anyone on the cable network.

Vitale was the athletic director at the University of Detroit when I first met him during Earvin's freshman year. The Spartans were scheduled to play the Titans at Calihan Hall in December, 1977, and Gus Ganakas and I called the game that night on local television.

We drove to the game together and arrived early enough to meet with Vitale, whom Gus knew from his earlier coaching days. Vitale's former assistant, Smokey Gaines, had taken over as the Detroit head coach, and Vitale was trying any promotion he could think of to help fill his arena. Bringing Magic Johnson and the Spartans to town that night filled Calihan Hall with no problem.

Vitale couldn't have been nicer, and we shared a few laughs over a couple of hours of conversation in his office during the afternoon. Vitale's enthusiasm and passion for his mission then was the same as it is when he describes a game on the air today. I made a comment to Gus after we left that he still tells others about today.

"How'd you like him, Tim?" Gus asked as we were leaving.

"My ears are hoarse," I exclaimed, without even thinking about a line to use in describing that first acquaintance.

Vitale has been a loyal friend of mine ever since. He lives in Sarasota, Florida, where my family spends the winter, and whenever I am there we try to get together. Whenever he calls a Spartans game, I'll try to help him with some advance notes that he might not otherwise come across. And he's been great to me with countless guest spots on my daily radio show.

The night the Spartans played at Detroit, Vitale decided to have a wild introduction of the Titans' players—complete with a darkened gym, laser lights, wild music, and all that goes with current NBA introductions of today. And he indeed did fire up the crowd. But the Spartans put on a clinic that night and blew the host team out of the game early. Earvin showed the Detroit area fans that indeed a magical college career had been born in East Lansing.

—*Tim Staudt*

A Bitter Pill to Swallow

The University of Michigan had outstanding basketball teams in the mid-1970s and was clearly better than Michigan State.

However, when 1977-78 rolled around and veterans Bob Chapman and Gregory Kelser were joined by freshmen Mike Brkovich, Earvin Johnson and Jay Vincent, things were sure to change.

Not so!

Mark Lozier hit a jumper at the buzzer from the top of the key that gave the Wolverines their sixth straight win over the Spartans, five since Kelser donned the green and white.

"I'll never forget Johnny Orr [Michigan's antimated head coach] running out of Jenison blowing kisses to our fans," Kelser said. "I had so looked forward to beating these guys that I felt like quitting."

The skid came to an end the following week when the Spartans went to Crisler Arena and posted a convincing 73-62 triumph.

"I kept myself on an even keel in preparation for that game," Kelser recalled. "I wasn't about to get way up and then crash if we lost.

"The funny thing was that when we kicked their butts like we did, there wasn't the exhilaration I was hoping for. It was just another win."

It Must Be Magic

I had watched Earvin Johnson's "Magic Show" close up for three years at Lansing Everett, and I still didn't realize how good the big fella was.

Any doubts I may have had were put to rest early in his freshman season for Michigan State.

The Spartans started out 5-1, winning the five games by an average of 21 points.

MSU lost its only real test (game No. 3) in the finals of the Carrier Classic to host Syracuse, 75-67.

Despite the loss, Johnson was named the tourney MVP.

In my mind, the telltale game was the win at Detroit in the seventh game of the young campaign. The Titans were undefeated and ranked in the top 10 in the country.

Historic Calihan Hall was packed to the rafters to root on future NBA players wearing red and white like Terry Duerod, John Long and Terry Tyler.

Few outside of the Spartan basketball family figured MSU had much of a chance. Heck, the Titans had won the previous two games including a 99-94 decision in Jenison Field House a year before.

However, when the last dunk ripped through the cords and the final no-look pass from Magic had found its mark, the scoreboard read: Michigan State 103, Detroit 74.

What had happened in one short year?

Senior guard Bob Chapman, a member of Jud Heathcote's first team that went 10-17 in 1976-77, summed it up best as he headed off the floor.

"It must be Magic," Chapman said with a smile from ear to ear.

—Fred Stabley Jr.

He Who Laughs Last...

The bus from the hotel to the basketball arena in Jacksonville, Fla., was well under way when a look of alarm crossed the face of Ron Charles.

"What's the matter?" asked his roommate and close friend, Gregory Kelser.

"I forgot my shoes," Charles said, slowly.

His response immediately set off an uproar of laughter by his Spartan teammates, Kelser included.

All of a sudden, Kelser stopped laughing.

"It just dawned on me that I didn't have mine, either," Kelser said. "Ron immediately perked up because he wasn't alone.

"They sent somebody back to our room, and we got the expected long lecture from Jud [Heathcote]."

A Dark Moment in a Bright Career

It's funny how bad things often stick in your mind more so than all the good things that may have happened to you.

Such is the case with Terry Donnelly when he took a moment to think back on his four-year career for Michigan State.

"One thing I'll never forget is a game at Michigan in my freshman year and we had the game won," Donnelly said. "Michigan was No. 1 in the country, but we were ahead by four or six points late in the game."

All the Spartans had to do was get the ball down the floor and waste some time.

Not to be.

The Wolverines' super-quick guard Ricky Greene stole the ball from the young freshman guard and went in for a dunk. MSU got the ball in, and Greene swiped it again from Donnelly and dunked it.

Ron "Bobo" Charles was a slender leaper for the Spartans who had one of his best games in the green and white against a physical Louisiana State team. The 6'8" product of the Virgin Islands had 18 points and 14 rebounds in the 87-71 NCAA tourney win. *Photo courtesy of MSU Sports Information*

The momentum changed and Michigan went on to claim a 69-66 overtime win.

"I realized what the rivalry was about then," Donnelly said. "I pretty much lost the game for us. That was a pretty horrible moment.

"I'd guarded a lot of players like Isiah Thomas and Ronnie Lester, but Greene was the quickest from end to end I'd ever seen. How he stole those balls, I'll never know."

CHAPTER 3

The Championship Season

Quite a Trip to Brazil

Gerald Gilkie found Michigan State's preseason basketball excursion to Brazil nearly as enjoyable as the Spartans' run to the 1979 NCAA championship.

The 6'5" walk-on forward from Detroit Kettering High saw extended playing time on the trip and took advantage of sightseeing opportunities whenever possible.

"I got a lot more playing time in Brazil than I did the rest of the season," Gilkie said.

"It was a lot of fun, and I actually played pretty well."

Gilkie and assistant coach Bill Berry got to see what the rest of the world calls "football" and Americans refer to as "soccer."

"There were 100,000 or 200,000 people in the stadium chanting in unison," Gilkie said. "It was pretty amazing, quite an experience."

Gilkie also recalled how everywhere they went the Brazilians would always come up to them and ask, "Which one is JOHN-sun?"

"It may have been Brazil, but they'd heard of Earvin Johnson," Gilkie said.

A Cowboy Hat and a Reprieve

Gregory Kelser turned 21 when the Spartans were in Brazil playing in two basketball tournaments in the summer prior to his senior season.

Jud Heathcote gave him a cowboy hat as a present, but Kelser liked what the third-year MSU head coach told him even more.

"I'm not going to be on you anymore," Heathcote said.

"Because I'm a senior," Kelser responded.

"That's part of it," Heathcote answered. "If you don't know what I want by now, you never will."

Kelser walked away with a smile on his face.

"It was a tremendous hurdle crossed," Kelser said.

Kelser and his Spartan teammates defeated Brazil, one of the premier amateur teams in the world, on the trip.

"That's when I started thinking we were good enough to win it all," he said. "There were a lot of teams feeling the same way like Duke, Arkansas and Kansas, though.

"When we beat the Russians at home, and beat them handily, I think that elevated us from the rest of the pack."

"Criminal Injustice"

While the 1978-79 Michigan State basketball team could handle most of its opposition on the floor, off the court was sometimes a different situation.

Gerald Gilkie was a criminal justice major at MSU and a walk-on member of the basketball team.

He got a close up look at criminal "injustice" during the Spartans' trip to Brazil in the summer of 1978 when a pickpocket took his wallet with "at least $20" in it.

Gilkie got the wallet back but not the money.

"A heavy-set women bumped into me and then this little kid starts running away," Gilkie recalled.

"She must have taken my wallet and then passed it off to the kid. A little while later a little kid came back and handed me my wallet ... without the money.

"I could speak a little Spanish, but they spoke Portuguese, so I didn't want to make a big deal out of it. I got my wallet back, which mattered the most."

Another unnerving situation that the Spartans faced was a bomb scare phoned in during the first half of the Jan. 11 game at the University of Illinois.

"I remember quite clearly the announcement by the public address announcer advising everyone of the bomb threat," said MSU reserve forward Rick Kaye. "It was kind of an uneasy feeling sitting on the bench, I'll tell you that."

Few of the 16,209 fans left the jam-packed Assembly Hall, opting to watch the Illini run their record to 15-0 and end Michigan State's reign as the No. 1 team in the land, 57-55.

Televising the Magical Spartans

One of the great thrills I enjoyed early in my career was calling high school basketball games on the radio. And when the Everett Vikings and Magic Johnson were playing, fans listened to the games in the mid-Michigan area because the gyms were always sold out.

In the middle 1970s, local television stations were just developing their hardware. Videotape news cameras were not in use yet, and neither were satellite trucks. There was no cable television yet, either. The notion of a local television station airing

Gerald Gilkie, who works as a counselor at the Ionia State Prison, lost $20 when a pickpocket relieved him of his wallet during MSU's trip to Brazil. *Photo courtesy of MSU Sports Information*

its own version of live sporting events in a market the size of Lansing just wasn't realistic.

But we had received permission to carry live the 1977 Class A district tournament opening game from Eastern High School's Don Johnson Fieldhouse. Because the old WJIM-TV studio was less than a mile away from the game site, we found that we could get a live picture hookup with the equipment we did have. We had no trouble selling the broadcast to sponsors, and it was a big deal. Earvin's team knocked Jay's Eastern Quakers out on the opening night, 63-41, and it was Jay Vincent's final prep appearance. We had no technical glitches, which was phenomenal in my mind, since all of our people involved with the telecast had no experience with such a production.

The afternoon that Earvin announced he would attend Michigan State, I raced into the office of my boss, WJIM-TV owner Harold F. Gross. I suggested we should broadcast the MSU basketball games. He agreed.

"I think many people would enjoy listening to the games on radio," he said. "We shouldn't have any problem getting sponsors."

But that wasn't what I had in mind.

"No, I'm talking about television. We've shown we could do the Eastern vs. Everett game—let's carry the Spartans on TV! We could do it!"

We sold Michigan State on the idea for a very nominal rights fee because we told the school officials we were doing them a favor. Since Jenison would be sold out with 10,000 fans, many more would be unable to see the games. By televising them, we would be relieving some of the MSU officials' ticket pressure.

We carried ten games during the 1977-78 season and eleven more the following year. We used our own crew of employees, and we chartered a bus that took all of us to road games. Most of the telecasts were Big Ten games, and our ratings were absolutely phenomenal. Remember there was no ESPN in those days and the number of college basketball games televised live across America in those days wasn't anything close to what it is today.

We never had one on-air glitch. We didn't have all the fancy picture equipment that is available and in wide use today, but we finally added a replay machine, and I thought we looked pretty good.

I went on to broadcast Big Ten basketball for the conference's network after cable television exploded in the 1980s and '90s— but I never enjoyed myself as much as I did those two years with the Magical Spartans.

My station was a hero to the community because we provided them free access to these marvelous Michigan State players. And I've always believed that because more people got to watch them play on local television, more fans were created and thus the frenzy for Earvin, Jay, and Special K continued to grow through that marvelous two-year period.

—*Tim Staudt*

Not Once but Twice

Donnie and Mike Brkovich had car trouble and were late in picking up Mike Longaker for the trip back to East Lansing where the Michigan State basketball team was congregating for a flight to Las Vegas and the 1979 Holiday Classic.

By the time the trio pulled into Capital City Airport, the flight had departed.

"Mike and I were seniors, and I knew we were going to hear about this one," Longaker said.

They waited around and caught the next flight out to Chicago.

The only problem was that they got confused and deplaned in Milwaukee.

"We were walking through the airport, and Donnie made some comment about the weather in Chicago," Longaker said. "Somebody overheard us and told us we were in Milwaukee.

"So we missed our second flight of the day. It was not a pleasant situation. One of the assistants picked us up when we got to Las Vegas. I don't remember much more about it, although I'm sure Jud [Heathcote] had something to say."

A First on the First

Michigan State may have played its finest basketball of the 1979 season—next to its romp through the NCAA tourney—at the Far West Classic in Jud Heathcote's triumphant return to the Northwest.

The Spartans destroyed his alma mater, Washington State, by a 98-52 margin in the opener, tripped Oregon State (65-57) in the second game and strolled by Indiana (74-57) in the championship tilt—the first of a remarkable three wins that season over Bob Knight's Hoosiers.

MSU left the Memorial Coliseum in Portland, Ore., with a 9-1 mark and thoughts of getting back to East Lansing for New Year's Eve. With losses by Duke, UCLA and Notre Dame, there was also the chance the Spartans could begin 1979 ranked No. 1.

One out of two isn't bad.

A terrible snowstorm hit the Midwest, and the farthest the Spartans could get was Denver, where they celebrated New Year's Eve sleeping in a motel. On New Year's Day, the weary travelers made it to Minneapolis and watched bowl games the rest of the day.

Heathcote called a team meeting the next day and said that they'd fly to Detroit and then bus home.

In typical Jud fashion, he added: "In case any of you in the room are interested, all of you are a part of the No. 1 basketball team in America."

It marked the first time in 80 years of Michigan State basketball that it was ever ranked No. 1 in the country.

Police Escort

Darwin Payton couldn't believe his eyes when Jud Heathcote hopped on the conveyor belt and disappeared into the bowels of Metro Airport looking for Michigan State's luggage.

"It was at the end of an endless trip back from the Far West Classic, and the luggage was slow in getting out," said Payton, a manager for the Spartans. "So Jud got on the belt and just disappeared through the flaps.

"I'd seen a lot of funny things in my life, but that may have topped them all."

That was rivaled minutes later when Jud was escorted out from behind the baggage area by the police.

"Any other place than Detroit, he'd have been arrested," Payton said. "But he was pretty well known and they just let him go."

When Jenison Was Quiet

People have asked Mike Brkovich more about one game than any other during the 1978-79 NCAA championship season at Michigan State.

And it wasn't the win over Indiana State in the finals.

It was the 83-72 overtime victory against Iowa, a game in which the "Wizard from Windsor" forced the extra five minutes by sinking two free throws with three seconds remaining and the Spartans trailing 65-63.

"Jenison Field House was always so loud, and when I stepped to the line, there was dead silence," Brkovich said. "Iowa called a timeout or two, and each time in the huddle Jud [Heathcote] would talk about what we were going to do after I made the free throws.

"Just as I was leaving the huddle before the final free throw, Coach told me 'You'll make it.'"

Heathcote was right, although Brkovich doesn't remember much about either free throw.

"They went in," Brkovich said. "I was nervous. I hadn't been playing a lot up until then."

Heathcote said that both were "swishes" but laughed when he recalled Brkovich in the postgame interview. "Somebody asked him about the second free throw and Brk said, 'What second free throw?'"

That Brkovich even had the opportunity to tie the game on his desperation shot from the top of the key was controversial for the Hawkeyes. Iowa coach Lute Olson maintained that Mike took steps prior to the shot, and others felt the foul on Ronnie Lester shouldn't have been called.

Ever the diplomat, Brkovich now looks at it this way: "It probably wouldn't have been a foul early in the game, but at the end with the game on the line the referee had no choice."

The foul was Lester's fifth, and Iowa missed him in the extra period as the Spartans pulled away for the Big Ten win that raised their conference mark to 4-2.

There Were Some Bumps in the Road

It wasn't all smooth sailing for Michigan State during its run to the 1979 NCAA championship.

In fact, Gregory Kelser remembers the bus trip home from Purdue after a 52-50 setback, coming on the heels of a 57-55 loss at Illinois two days earlier.

Coach Jud Heathcote was not in the best mood to begin with. But young adults are always more resilient, and the Spartan players recovered quickly.

One of the players was playing music, and Jud hollered out: "Cut the music!"

Out with the music … in with the singing.

"Cut the singing," bellowed Heathcote.

The singing stopped and the whistling began.

"Cut the whistling," yelled the angry coach.

Soon, the players were humming.

"Cut the humming," Jud stormed.

And the humming disappeared.

It was quiet for a second, when Kelser started in with Martin Luther King's famous "Dream Speech."

"I had just seen a movie on Martin Luther King," Kelser said. "It was the wrong thing to do, but we were angry we lost, and heads butted. We drew a line, and he did, too. We were anti-everything that night."

The remainder of the trip was quiet, but Kelser knew it wasn't over.

At practice the next day, Heathcote gathered the troops.

"If anybody here thinks they're tougher than me, stand up," Heathcote said. "Does anybody think they're tougher than any of these coaches?"

The room was stone quiet.

"I believe if anybody had moved, Jud would have tackled them," Spartan forward Ron Charles said.

Heathcote went on to say that that type of insubordination would not happen again. Period!

"Jud could have suspended a bunch of us that night, but he elected to let it ride and handle it the next day," Kelser said. "In effect, he backed us all down. He certainly made his point."

"The Meeting"

M ick McCabe just calls it "The Meeting."
Currently the prep sports guru for the *Detroit Free Press*, also known as the Son of Swami, the bearded one was a beat reporter covering Michigan State basketball in 1979.

He stumbled on an interesting story following MSU's NCAA-opening win over Lamar.

"A couple of reporters corralled Earvin [Johnson] in a hallway away from everyone else," McCabe recalled.

"This team was heading south midway through the Big Ten season, and only one conference team was guaranteed an NCAA bid.

"We were asking him about the big turnaround when Earvin mentioned a players-only meeting followed by one with the coaches earlier in the season. The gist of the whole thing was that the players said they'd play harder if the coaches got off their backs."

The meeting took place on the Monday after the Spartans' Big Ten record fell to 4-4 with an 83-65 loss at lowly

Northwestern. MSU proceeded to win 10 straight games to grab the Big Ten's automatic NCAA bid.

"I wrote the story for the next day's paper, and Jud [Heathcote] was so mad he wouldn't talk to me," McCabe recalled. "I told him I got everything verbatim from Earvin, but it didn't matter."

Mike Brkovich didn't consider the meeting quite as pivotal in the season as others might have.

"It was a venting meeting," Brkovich said. "I didn't think it was that big a deal. I didn't notice that much of a difference in the coaching ... maybe a little less yelling, but only a little. We just had to play more together to salvage the season."

Heathcote came away from the meeting with the realization that a change in the lineup was needed.

"We benched Ron Charles, who had been playing well, in favor of another guard in Brkovich," Heathcote said. "Our Big Ten opponents had taken away the fast break by putting a man on Earvin when we would get the ball.

"We needed another ball handler, and we could get that by going to Terry Donnelly or Brkovich if Earvin was covered. We had to do something, because the Big Ten was only guaranteed one NCAA berth, and there was a definite sense of urgency."

While Jud may not have thought the meeting was that pivotal, Earvin felt it was crucial.

"Everybody got something different out of it," he said. "It was the best thing for me, personally. We were playing basketball like they used to play it in the 1950s and '60s, and not running and having fun like we were capable of.

"Jud loosened up a bit, and everybody relaxed. We came together as a team. I think there was a lot of pressure on us being ranked No. 1 in the country. The pressure from within was off, and we all loosened up."

The Spartans responded by ripping off 10 straight wins, and 15 in their final 16 outings.

The first two games after the meeting were hard-fought home victories over Ohio State (84-79) in overtime and Northwestern (61-50). Victories, but nothing special.

The day after the Northwestern win, Michigan State smashed a pretty solid Kansas team, 85-61, in Jenison.

"That game turned everything around for us," Johnson said. "The crowd was roaring, we were running and dunking, and we left that game convinced we were back on track."

It came right in time, too, as the next three games were on the road at Iowa, Ohio State, and Indiana. MSU won the three by more than 10 points per game, and never looked back.

Back from the "Dead"

It's probably the most fabled ankle sprain in Michigan State history, and one of the first people on the scene was veteran trainer Clint Thompson.

The Spartans were rolling in a must-win game with Ohio State, holding a 32-23 lead late in the first half when Earvin Johnson hit the floor writhing in pain. Seldom had Jenison Field House been so quiet as the throng of 10,004 held their collective breaths.

The Buckeyes entered the game with an 8-0 Big Ten record while the struggling Spartans were only 4-4 in conference action. Another loss would almost certainly ruin any chances MSU had of capturing the Big Ten crown and earning an NCAA bid.

"Even though he was in obvious pain, Earvin was adamant that he wasn't hurt that badly," Thompson recalled.

Dr. David Hough, team physician, and Thompson took Johnson to the locker room and examined the ankle.

"We put it on ice and watched it for a period of time," Thompson said.

Meanwhile, the Spartan lead had disappeared and OSU moved into its first lead with 14:10 remaining in the game, 39-38.

"They'd already made up their mind that I wasn't going to play," Johnson said afterwards. "But I told them that there's no use holding me back because if we lost there was no tomorrow."

So they taped him up for a trial run in the hall outside the training room in the bowels of Jenison.

"If an athlete was functional, meaning he could run, cut and jump, then we'd give him a chance," Thompson said. "Earvin did enough for us to give him the okay.

"We may have been taking a slight chance, but we never would have let him go out there if he wasn't functional."

Jay Vincent was on the free throw line and MSU had regained the lead, 44-43, when Earvin "magically" reappeared.

The very walls of Jenison shook.

"I couldn't imagine what all the noise was about," Vincent said. "And then I turned around and saw Earvin. It gave everybody a lift."

Johnson still can't believe what he heard.

"It was absolutely the loudest I'd ever heard Jenison," Magic said.

By the time he was inserted into the lineup—head coach Jud Heathcote said that he waited only one-third of a second after getting the word from Thompson—the Spartan lead was 48-43 with 8:42 to go.

Michigan State would eventually win the game in overtime, 84-79, thanks to six points each by Mike Brkovich and Johnson and five by Gregory Kelser.

The Spartans would then tack on nine more wins in a row (eight in the Big Ten) to tie for the championship and reach the NCAA tourney.

"Looking back on it, Earvin may not have been hurt as badly as we thought," Thompson said. "He was seldom hurt, and a moderate injury of any kind was an insult to Earvin's persona."

Johnson credited the crowd for his quick recovery.

"My ankle didn't feel quite as bad when the fans started cheering," Johnson said.

It was a turning point in a magical season.

Right on the Money

Detroit *Free Press* reporter Mick McCabe and Michigan State assistant coach Dave Harshman were talking after the Spartans' impressive 85-61 win over Kansas on national TV.

It was MSU's third win in four days, coming on the heels of road losses at Michigan and Northwestern.

"If we make the NCAA tournament, that's the way we'll play," Harshman predicted after the stunning win over the Jayhawks. "People in the Big Ten are better prepared to play us because they've seen this group for two years. It will be new to everyone we play in the tournament."

Harshman's prediction was right on. Michigan State won the five NCAA games by an average of 21 points a game, the two closest coming in the regional finals against Notre Dame (80-68) and in the finals against Indiana State (75-64).

Kelser: Always a Gentleman

Referee Charles Fouty had just tossed the ball up to start Michigan State's final home game of the 1978-79 season against Illinois when his glasses were knocked from his head.

Everyone headed down the floor except for senior Gregory Kelser, who spotted Fouty's dilemma and raced back to pick up the glasses and hand them to the greatful referee.

It was a small act from a man with an abundance of class.

"Spartan Rules"

They were called the "Spartan Rules," and they were detested by the girlfriends of Michigan State's basketball players.

They were unwritten rules but etched in concrete, nonetheless.

When the Spartans went somewhere during the NCAA championship season, they went together ... without their girlfriends.

"We had no cliques," said Earvin Johnson. "When we went out, all 13 guys went. We'd all go out for a walk or to the movies or to Dooley's [a popular East Lansing hangout].

"It made us a team, and when we stepped on the court we knew we could count on each other. That made us tough to beat."

Not much on the dating front, but definitely tough to beat!

Spartan Freshman Was in Awe of Magic

Donnie Brkovich spent most of the 1978-79 basketball season on the bench as a 6'6" freshman reserve guard for Michigan State.

He loved every second of it.

"I was in awe of Earvin Johnson," Brkovich said. "To be able to watch him in practice and in games that season was special. He looked at the game from a different perspective than anybody else in college basketball.

"He was 6'8" and brought the ball up the court, and could see things that I don't think people even see to this day. I was as amazed as everyone was, and I saw him in practice each day."

Brkovich, younger brother of Mike, played three minutes in the semifinals against Pennsylvania and scored two points and grabbed a rebound.

"Playing in the Final Four was special, but it really didn't set in until years later. I take a lot of pride now in saying that I played on a national championship team."

Brkovich took off on his own after his sophomore season and landed at the University of New Mexico.

"I needed a change of scenery," he said. "I wanted a chance to start, which I did for two years. New Mexico had tremendous crowds and it was fun playing there."

Brkovich used his experience at Michigan State to make him a better player in Albuquerque.

"Jud Heathcote was an expert on shooting technique, and he always emphasized the importance of knowing your teammates and their abilities," he remembered. "That helped me a lot at New Mexico."

While the Lobos were a .500 team in his two years there, Donnie did average 12.0 points a game as a junior and 8.0 as a senior.

Brkovich tried to extend his basketball career by trying out for the Albuqueque Silvers of the CBA, but got cut.

He still loves playing a couple of times a week at a health club in his adopted hometown of Las Vegas.

There Was No Answer for Earvin

When Michigan State's fast break was in high gear, it was virtually unstoppable.

In fact, Gerald Gilkie used to chuckle when opponents would call time out.

"What adjustment could they make for a guy like Earvin Johnson?" Gilkie said, a reserve forward on the 1978-79 club. "He could rebound, lead the fast break, and distribute the ball like nobody else—and he was 6'8". They had no answer for it."

Gilkie also loved the Spartans' killer instinct.

"We won a lot of close games because we were a tough-minded team," said Gilkie. "But this team had the chemistry that allowed it to put the knockout punch on a team at any time."

Say What?

Spartans basketball coach Jud Heathcote was ranting and raving at halftime of Michigan State's 1978-79 regular-season finale at Wisconsin.

"We're getting killed on the boards," Heathcote hollered. "We must be down by 10 rebounds or more. Can't anybody get a rebound?"

Just then, a student manager walked up with a stat sheet.

Jud looked at it for a moment and shook his head. "It says we're one rebound up," Heathcote said in disbelief. "There must be a mistake."

In the dead silence of the locker room came a voice from the back: "Stats … don't … lie," said Greg "Boobie" Lloyd, a free-spirited reserve guard.

Heathcote looked up slowly from the stat sheet, glared toward the Lansing Eastern product and said to assistant coach Bill Berry, "Bill, get him out of here."

"We were all in shock," said Don Brkovich. "It's awfully funny now, but nobody could believe he said it at that time. Nobody reacted to what he said except for Gregory Kelser, who had a little smirk on his face."

Lloyd didn't recall the incident, but it wouldn't have surprised him if it did happen.

"I was kind of a free spirit and was always getting in Jud's doghouse," Lloyd said with a laugh.

While the Spartans did end up getting outrebounded in the 82-80 loss, Kelser snared 10 caroms to become Michigan State's No. 1 all-time rebounder, passing Jumpin' Johnny Green's total of 1,036.

Donnie Brkovich, younger brother of starting guard Mike Brkovich, has become a successful businessman in Las Vegas. *Photo courtesy of MSU Sports Information*

Mismatch:
Longaker vs. Magic

There was nobody in college basketball who could match the skills of Earvin "Magic" Johnson.

He was a 6'8", 210-pound guard who could do it all.

The chore of "trying" to guard Magic during practice at Michigan State was often the duty of 6'1", 182-pound Mike Longaker.

"I wasn't tall, but I was pretty strong," Longaker said. "But what a dilemma. If I played absolutely as well as possible, I would be completely dominated.

"If I didn't play well, I would be completely dominated and embarrassed, too."

The competitive nature of Magic was one thing that always stuck out for Longaker.

"If I started hitting some long jumpers in warmups, the next thing I knew, there was Earvin right next to me trying to match me," Longaker said. "It just reflected his incredible competitive nature."

Johnson and Longaker were on the same team in a preseason four-on-four game upstairs at Jenison Field House, and they'd won 10 or 12 straight games.

"I was whipped," Longaker said. "I might even have been over on the sidelines throwing up when Earvin hollered for me to get back on the floor.

"But that was Earvin. He was always pushing himself and others."

Mike Longaker had the unenviable task in practice of trying to do what nobody during Earvin Johnson's famed basketball career could do—guard him. Mike is now a doctor at Stanford University. *Photo courtesy of MSU Sports Information*

CHAPTER 4

The Postseason Run

Singing a Spartan Song

The late Lansing human relations director Dick Letts was an ardent MSU fan.

Dick loved the basketball team and attended the first-round games on a bus with other Spartan supporters headed for the NCAA tournament opening games in 1978 in Murfreesboro, Tennessee.

Letts had become close friends with Earvin Johnson and his family during his development through his early school years. Letts also fancied himself as somewhat of a songwriter.

Letts wrote a tune on the bus during the long ride to Tennessee entitled "It's a long way to Murfreesboro." He passed out the lyrics to everyone on the bus. The melody was similar to "It's a long way to Tiperary."

By the time the bus arrived at its destination, all the fans knew the words and sang it repeatedly to help while away the hours on the road.

Bad Move

L amar University circled the floor before its second-round NCAA regional tilt with Michigan State at Middle Tennessee State, and the Cardinal players held their index fingers high in the air, signaling No. 1.

MSU head coach Jud Heathcote was sitting by himself on the Spartan bench, and the Cardinal players made a special effort to wave their fingers in his direction.

Manager Darwin Payton went back into the locker room and told the Spartan players what Lamar had done.

"Lamar showed disrespect to Jud, and nobody disrespects our coach," Earvin Johnson said. "We went out and taught them a lesson in basketball."

The Spartans rolled to the regional finals with a 95-64 crush of Lamar.

It was a special game in more ways than one for reserve guard Jaimie Huffman.

"I'll never forget the look in the eyes of Earvin [Johnson], Gregory [Kelser], Ron [Charles], and Jay [Vincent] after Lamar did that," he said. "When you mess with the bull, you're going to get the horn."

Late in the game, Jaimie lost a sneaker and, thanks to broadcaster Al McGuire, forever became known as "Shoes" Huffman.

Baked Crow

B illy Tubbs, Lamar's glib head coach, dominated the media's attention during the first and second rounds of the Mideast Regionals in Murfreesboro, Tenn.

The running Cardinals upset Detroit in their first-round encounter, 93-85, and took an 88-point scoring average into a second-round showdown with Michigan State (the Spartans had a first-round bye).

"We're aiming to take care of the whole state of Michigan," the affable Tubbs said in a southern drawl. "People tell me Michigan State plays a matchup zone, and I tell them I don't even know what a matchup zone is."

That much proved to be true.

The Spartans completely shut off the Cardinal running attack en route to a 95-64 spanking in the Murphy Athletic Center at Middle Tennessee State.

"That's what you call a good ole country butt-whipping," Tubbs said afterwards. "We got outplayed, outcoached and outeverythinged. It really wasn't a fair fight. All Michigan State did was shoot layups and we had to rely on jump shots."

MSU coach Jud Heathcote chuckled when he recalled Tubbs's postgame press conference. "Billy comes walking in, tearing up a report he got from a scouting service," Jud recalled. "He said, 'That's the last time I'm using that service. If Michigan State is a walk-up, non-fast-break team, I didn't see it.'"

Tubbs remained one of the top offensive coaches in the country for the next three decades, his last coaching job with the high-scoring Horned Frogs of Texas Christian University.

A Closer Look

B illy Tubbs told his players before the NCAA regional game with Michigan State in Murfreesboro, Tenn., that they'd better watch Magic Johnson.

"At the half, the players came into the locker room and said that we're watching him, and he's playing a helluva game," Tubbs said after his team dropped a 95-64 game at Middle Tennessee State.

Johnson had a typical evening with a triple double—17 rebounds, 13 points and 10 assists.

Tubbs also should have warned his Cardinals about Gregory Kelser, who had 31 points and 14 rebounds.

A Bad Break

J ay Vincent could not hide the disappointment of his limited role in Michigan State's run through the NCAA basketball tourney.

He broke the fourth metatarsal in his right foot in a first-round win over Lamar and played only 34 minutes and scored 21 points in the four games he got into.

"It was definitely my biggest setback on the collegiate level," Vincent said. "It was a chance to shine on a national level, but it didn't happen.

"I don't question why. I just had to get around it. I could have hung my head, or picked my head up and move on. I chose not to dwell on it."

Winning made it a tad easier.

"As long as we won, that was the main thing," Vincent said. "It was an unreal feeling. People were hollering everywhere outside of our hotel after the game."

Vincent had surgery on his foot during the off season and had a new procedure that had only been tried on former UCLA great Bill Walton.

"They drilled a hole in my foot and put in electrodes," Vincent said. "It helped heal the bone. I've had no problem with it since, which is pretty amazing because I'm a big guy and these feet took a lot of pounding."

When Jaimie Became "Shoes"

M ichigan State was in the process of blowing Lamar all the way back to Beaumont, Texas in the opening-round game of the 1979 NCAA championship run when Jud Heathcote cleared his bench.

A reserve guard from Lansing Everett, Jaimie Huffman, was among the eager Spartans to take the floor in Murfreesboro, Tenn.

Jaimie Huffman became a national celebrity during Michigan State's 1979 run to the national title when he lost a shoe in a cameo appearance against Lamar. Dick Enberg (left) and the late Al McGuire had fun interviewing "Shoes" later in the tourney. *Photo courtesy of MSU Sports Information*

In Huffman's opening seconds of action, a Lamar player stepped on his gym shoe and his heel came out.

"I wore low-cuts and tied my laces in a double knot so that they wouldn't come off," Huffman recalled with a chuckle. "The game was going on and I was trying to get my laces undone.

"Jud was hollering at me to run down the floor without the shoe, and I tried but it was like I was on ice. So I just took my time and got it done."

However, NBC commentator Al McGuire started counting players as the two teams raced up and down the floor and discovered one missing. He looked at one end of the floor and found Jaimie busy at work.

McGuire immediately started calling him "Shoes" Huffman.

"It was a blowout, and he was looking for something to spice up the game," said Huffman.

Moments later, Huffman scored his first basket of the season, and on a subsequent free throw attempt the television cameras zeroed in on Jaimie's … shoes.

"When we got back to East Lansing, there was a sign on the dorm that read 'Welcome Home Shoes' and the bookstore was selling 'Shoes' memorabilia," Huffman recalled.

Huffman played in the NCAA semis, a 101-67 romp over Pennsylvania, and he made one spectacular behind-the-back pass for a basket by Rick Kaye.

"I don't remember exactly, but let's just say that Rick dunked it," Huffman said laughing. "It makes it sound better."

Huffman was in the locker room after that game when Michigan State SID Fred Stabley said he was wanted back on the floor to be interviewed.

"I thought it was a newspaper or something," he said. "But when I got to the floor, it was Dick Enberg and McGuire, and I was live on NBC. That was pretty incredible."

So, whatever happened to those shoes?

"My brother, Damon, wore them and I guess they got misplaced," Huffman said. "It would have been kind of neat to make a pair of book ends out of them."

Huffman's roommate on the road was Gerald Gilkie, and he gave Jaimie a lot of good-natured grief over all the attention he was getting.

"Gerald said he was going to pull his shorts down the next time he played and people were going to starting calling him 'Shorts,'" Huffman said, laughing.

Bobo Was Awesome

Ron "Bobo" Charles will never be confused with Lou Gehrig, and Jay Vincent was not Wally Pipp.

But for one game, anyway, with the help of some pregame music from his teammates, Bobo was the man.

"Earvin [Johnson] started singing a version of a song by Lakeside called 'All the Way Live,'" Charles said. "But Earvin changed the lyrics to 'All the Way Bobo.'

"Pretty soon everybody on the bus was singing it, and I got pretty pumped up."

With Vincent sidelined with a bum foot, Charles returned to the starting lineup—a spot he'd occupied for the first 19 games until Michigan State went to a smaller and better-shooting unit with Mike Brkovich as a starter.

However, in a physical and incredibly intense game with Louisiana State, the reed-thin and mild-mannered Charles came up big. He had 18 points and a career-high 14 rebounds to lead MSU to an 87-71 win.

"It was probably my best game," said the quiet man with the distinct accent from his native Virgin Islands. "I had three dunks early in the game, and then I started grabbing rebounds all over the place. As the game went on, I just felt better and better."

Charles did start all five NCAA tourney games and averaged 9.6 points and 6.8 rebounds to become one of the Spartans' numerous unsung heroes.

Digger

Digger Phelps still resides in South Bend, Indiana, despite the fact that he stepped down in 1991 after 20 seasons as head basketball coach at Notre Dame. He joined ESPN in 1993, and while that is what he is most known for these days, he had plenty of success coaching the Fighting Irish.

Former Notre Dame coach Digger Phelps meets the media after his Fighting Irish lost in the regional finals to Michigan State in Indianapolis. He felt the winner would capture the 1979 NCAA crown. *Photo courtesy of MSU Sports Information*

Phelps was 37 years old when his team met Michigan State in the 1979 Mideast Regional championship game in nearby Indianapolis. Digger felt the winner of that game would go on to win the NCAA championship because he felt both the Spartans and his Irish were capable of beating unbeaten Indiana State in the championship game.

Notre Dame fielded a marvelous team against the Spartans that Sunday afternoon at Market Square Arena, which has since been demolished. You'll recognize many of the names—Bill Laimbeer, Kelly Tripucka, Tracy Jackson, Bill Hanzlik, Orlando Woolridge, and Rich Branning.

One day after St. Patrick's Day, March 18, 1979, a capacity crowd of 17,423 roared from the opening tip when Mike Brkovich, off a setup play, scored on a dunk in the first three seconds of the game. The Spartans arguably played their best game of the entire season that afternoon.

"Kelser killed us," Phelps said nearly 25 years later. And he did. On 15-for-25 shooting, Kelser scored 34 points and pulled down 13 rebounds. Michigan State shot 63 percent in the second half and 57.4 percent for the entire game.

"We just couldn't stop Kelser, and then you add the fact that Johnson had 19 points and 13 assists, and it was just too much for us," Phelps adds.

Since Phelps now gets paid to analyze teams and players, the obvious questions to him are: Was the '79 team the best of all the NCAA champions?

"All championship teams are great teams," is as far as he'll go. He'll cite other great NCAA title-winning teams and name the '79 Spartans in the same breath.

And how would the '79 team compare with the 2000 championship MSU team, Digger?

"Both were great teams—because both won national championships even though they each did it in different ways."

Phelps admired Jud Heathcote in 1979 much the way he admires Tom Izzo today.

"Izzo is meant for college basketball," Phelps told an audience during a speech in East Lansing in 2002. "He's a great teacher."

After the Spartans beat his Irish in 1979, Phelps stopped Kelser when he was leaving the floor in the final moments of the game. He encouraged him to stay focused since he knew the Spartans were the odds-on favorite to win two more games at the Final Four.

After the game that day in Indianapolis, Phelps said, "Michigan State's players know each other so well and complement each other in so many different ways. The great thing about the coaching job Jud has done is to make them play disciplined and organized basketball, but yet let them have the freedom to be themselves."

The loss was a disappointment for Phelps, whose 1978 team made the Final Four and whose '79 team had the veterans and future NBA stars he felt could win the title which Michigan State instead captured. The Spartans' defeat of Notre Dame left that Irish team with a 24-7 record and years to consider what might have been.

Change of Venue

The NCAA assigns hotels to the teams who compete in basketball's NCAA tournament each year. But in the 1979 regionals at Indianapolis, Notre Dame coach Digger Phelps changed hotels the night before the game against Michigan State.

It seems the Spartans' pep band kept playing on the balconies and creating all kinds of noise, and the wild MSU fans kept cheering them on. After a couple of nights of the partying, Phelps had heard enough. The Irish moved out before losing the game the next day.

We're Not That Skinny!

Three of Michigan State's four 6'8" standouts on the 1979 NCAA championship basketball team didn't have any extra body weight to throw around.

In fact, a pregame story in the *Indianapolis Star* before the Spartans' 80-68 win over Notre Dame may have provided a little incentive for the green and white.

"The gist of the story was that we had no beef up front and there was no way we could handle Bill Laimbeer, Notre Dame's 6'11", 260-pound center," said Ron Charles.

The story listed Earvin Johnson as 6'8" and 190 pounds, Gregory Kelser 6'8" and 175 and Charles 6'8" and 172.

"It kind of got us mad," Charles recalled. "I was skinny, but not 172 pounds."

By the way, the future Detroit Pistons star Laimbeer had seven points and four rebounds for the Irish, while Kelser finished with 34 and 13, Johnson 19 and five with 13 assists, and Charles had six and four.

Spartans Were Ready for Fighting Irish

When Michigan State's bus pulled up to Market Square Arena, the players had a perfect view of Market Street.

What they saw went a long way in getting them pumped up for their NCAA regional final showdown with Notre Dame.

"All we could see was a wave of green and white coming down the street, Spartan fans everywhere," Earvin "Magic" Johnson recalled. "We got goose bumps all over. Man, we got excited. We knew Notre Dame was in trouble."

The Spartans proceeded to their locker room and began getting dressed. As usual, Magic had the music blasting.

When the door opened a little while later and Jud Heathcote walked in, Earvin immediately shut off the music. It was time for Jud's pregame talk.

"Put the music back on," Jud said. "We don't have anything more to go over. Let's just go out there and kick their ass."

Magic agreed.

"Jud did a great job preparing us the day before," he said. "We were fired up for this game. I was so keyed up that I couldn't sleep the night before."

Always looking for an edge, Jud made a big deal out of the fact that Notre Dame refused to come to East Lansing that year to play a nationally televised game with the Spartans.

"It was just something else to get us riled up about," Magic said.

In preparing for the Irish, Heathcote noticed that Notre Dame did not keep a man back on the opening tip. Jud came up with a play where Gregory Kelser would get the tip to Earvin who would then pass it to a breaking Mike Brkovich for a layup.

"Before the opening tip, I told Brk to dunk it," Earvin said. "It would get the crowd going.

"Gregory got it to me and I just tapped it over my head and started down the floor the other way. I didn't even look. But I heard. We sent a message early on."

It was a recurring message as the Spartans dunked their way into the Final Four with an 80-68 win.

A Special Spartan

Among MSU basketball fans, few are like Duane Vernon. The former head of the Greater Lansing Credit Bureau was featured in *Sports Illustrated* magazine several years ago as one of the top college sports fans in America. Jud Heathcote even called him on the phone the following week to tease him about his national publicity and growing reputation.

Duane lives with his wife, Judy, in the Mar Moor subdivision of Lansing, some ten miles from the MSU campus. The basement of his home is legendary in Spartan circles. It has a bar shaped like an S and the thick green carpet covers all of the floors. The walls are adorned with numerous MSU artifacts, framed pictures, and stories, many depicting the exploits of the 1979 team and season.

Gregory "Special K" Kelser rips down a rebound in front of Orlando Woolridge in Michigan State's convincing 80-68 regional title romp over Notre Dame in Indianapolis's Market Square Arena. *Photo courtesy of MSU Sports Information*

The Vernons have held gala Super Bowl parties for years in which several hundred people spread around their house to view the game on rented television sets scattered throughout. And the same scenario worked wonders on the night of the 1979 NCAA championship telecast. Some 375 fans watched the game at the Vernons' and even the *Today Show* sent a camera crew to record all of the excitement.

It was Duane Vernon who hastily assembled a committee to plan the celebratory parade for when the Spartans returned home from Salt Lake City. Duane is still active in planning parades in the Greater Lansing area, but the one he helped organize to welcome home the 1979 champions still stands above all the rest in terms of excitement and attendance. I was on the committee. I marched in the front of the parade. I can attest to the fact, and so can Duane, that more people were present on the streets of downtown Lansing to welcome home the '79 team than the number who were involved in the parade honoring the 2000 champions.

While Duane Vernon did not attend the Final Four in Salt Lake City, he did make the trip to Indianapolis for the regionals. The Sunday final game against Notre Dame will never leave his memory.

"MSU owned Indianapolis that day," he recalls. "Notre Dame never had a chance. Thousands of fans marched from the Civil War monument downtown to the arena. They were all singing and chanting the MSU fight song. It was an incredible scene.

"What people forget about that season is how hard it was to get into the tournament in those days. There were 48 teams involved then instead of today's 64. And only two teams made it from the Big Ten. We were so fortunate just to make the field after the start to the Big Ten season we had."

Still vitally active in many community endeavors today, Duane Vernon's green and white loyalty 25 years ago assured him that his beloved Spartans would win the national title.

"Once we got in, I knew we were going to win it all."

—*Tim Staudt*

Dunk You Very Much

One of my favorite tales from the Spartans' storybook run to the NCAA title happened against Notre Dame in Market Square Arena in the Mideast Regional Finals.

A young MSU fan dressed in his best green and white sat next to an equally loyal and fired-up Irish booster.

Some good-natured kidding ensued with the youngster promising that his beloved Spartans would have five or six dunks before the game was over.

"I'll bet you $5 that Michigan State doesn't even get one dunk," the Notre Dame fan said.

The young boy looked at his father, who nodded his okay, and the bet was on.

Well, on the game's opening tap, Gregory Kelser tipped it forward to Earvin Johnson who just batted it over his head to a streaking Mike Brkovich.

Dunk! Bet over! Bet paid!

Even though MSU ended up with a number of additional dunks, the first one was not even supposed to happen. Jud Heathcote gave Brkovich explicit instructions to lay the ball in … not dunk it.

"We saw that Notre Dame didn't put anybody back," Heathcote recalled. "We had Brkovich going and we hoped that Gregory would get the tip to Earvin. As usual, Mike didn't listen to me. He had to dunk it."

Brkovich recalled the play with a chuckle.

"It was Earvin or Gregory who told me to go up and dunk the ball," Brkovich said. "I knew it was a big game, maybe the NCAA championship game a week early, and it would give us a lift more than a layup would.

"Jud never said a word to me afterwards."

—*Fred Stabley Jr.*

On One Foot

Two things that are often overlooked in Michigan State's 1979 NCAA playoff run were: one, that the Spartans won the five postseason games by an average of 20.8 points; and two, they did it virtually without 6'8" sophomore Jay Vincent being a major factor.

Jay played in only four of those games because of a foot injury and scored just 21 points. He had injured the fat pad under his right big toe in the Big Ten finale at Wisconsin and tried to play through the pain by running on the side of his foot.

He then sustained a stress fracture in the lopsided win over Lamar and limped the rest of the way through the tournament.

Vincent didn't play against LSU, and the 19 minutes in the finale against Indiana State proved to be his most extended postseason playing time. He had five points and two rebounds against the Sycamores.

One basket in the regional finals was memorable for Spartan fans, though.

In his two and one-half minutes against Notre Dame, Vincent gave a head fake and hobbled around 6'11" future NBA standout Bill Laimbeer for an easy layup.

"Earvin [Johnson] and Gregory [Kelser] always talk about that one," Vincent said.

"That was my limping layup. It really wasn't that big a deal. Laimbeer was certain I was going to shoot the jumper because he didn't think I could move on the bad foot.

"Funny thing is that I couldn't have taken the jump shot on just one foot. I didn't have enough balance."

Playing against Laimbeer many times in the NBA, Vincent grew to respect his Fighting Irish foe.

"You talk about a smart basketball player and someone who was tough under the boards," Vincent said. "That was Bill Laimbeer."

Six Is Not Enough

No game during the 1979 NCAA basketball tournament was more anticipated or hyped than the Mideast Regional Finals in Indianapolis between Michigan State and Notre Dame.

As the 1978-79 season unfolded, it seemed as though a matchup between these two touted teams was inevitable.

While the game was hotly contested before 17,423 fans in Market Square Arena, the Spartans' quick start and overall quickness proved to be too much in an 80-68 win that sent the green and white faithful heading to Salt Lake City.

When Jud Heathcote looks back, he's convinced it was for the NCAA title.

"If Notre Dame would have beaten us, it would have won the championship," Heathcote said.

Star forward Gregory Kelser agreed.

"It was huge," he said. "Notre Dame was outstanding ... we felt it was for the national title. We respected our opponents in the Final Four, but we didn't think anybody had the talent Notre Dame did."

When you look back on it and saw what transpired in the years to come, MSU's win over the Irish is even more impressive. Notre Dame had six NBA players in its playing group—Bruce Flowers (one year in the NBA), Bill Hanzlik (11), Tracy Jackson (3), Bill Laimbeer (15), Kelly Tripucka (9), and Orlando Woolridge (13). A seventh player, Rich Branning, was drafted but did not make it.

The Spartans had three in Earvin "Magic" Johnson, Gregory Kelser, and Jay Vincent. Of course, EJ is considered one of the five greatest basketball players in history, which didn't hurt.

Not a Top 10 Hit

After Michigan State had defeated Notre Dame in the regional finals at Indianapolis's Market Square Arena, the Spartans were a giddy and loose group heading back home.

"We knew we were going to the Final Four and there was a lot of kidding and joking," recalled Rob Gonzalez (aka Roberto Gonzalez Narozny). "We were pretty ecstatic and we started singing a goofy song that singled out each player on the team.

"I remember quite well that I was the Mexican chili bean."

Gonzalez, a 6'7" freshman forward on the team, also remembered the tremendous competitive spirit that oozed from Magic Johnson and spilled over into his teammates.

"The spirit and will of Earvin to win carried that team to victory," Gonzalez said. "We had a motto because of that … 'refuse to lose.'"

After rolling to a 101-67 semifinal victory over Pennsylvania, a game in which Gonzalez played 22 minutes and scored two points and grabbed three rebounds, there was a quick turnaround for the title tilt with Indiana State.

"I was amazed at the businesslike approach we had at practice the next day and at our shootaround the day of the game," Gonzalez said. "The game was a direct extension of those two practices.

"Coach Heathcote instilled that mindset and made our team invincible that night."

A Quiet Confidence

Gregory Kelser never doubted for one moment that Michigan State would defeat Indiana State in the NCAA finals in 1979.

"We were on top of our game, and I really didn't see any way we could lose," Kelser said. "The simple fact of the matter was that teams outside of the Big Ten did not fare well against us."

Kelser had a point.

In the two years that Earvin Johnson, Jay Vincent, and Kelser played together at MSU, the Spartans were an incredible 23-3 against teams outside of the Big Ten.

And the three losses were by a total of 12 points—75-67 at Syracuse in 1977, 52-49 in the NCAA regional finals to Kentucky (in Dayton) in 1978 and 70-69 at North Carolina early in the 1978-79 campaign.

"We pummeled everyone else," Kelser said.

The 23 non-Big Ten wins in those two seasons came by an average of 21.3 points.

The closest margin of victory in 1977-78 was the season-opening 68-61 home triumph over Central Michigan, while in 1978-79 it was a 92-89 home nod over Cal State-Fullerton in the second game.

In a Sea of Green and White

Malcolm Moran had been at the *New York Times* less than three months when he was assigned to cover the 1979 NCAA basketball championships in Salt Lake City, Utah.

"I'll never forget the Friday afternoon shootaround," said Moran, who now writes for *USA Today* and hasn't missed a Final Four since. "There were probably five or six thousand people in the Special Events Center, and most of them were from Michigan State."

The Spartans were finishing their workout when someone threw down a dunk.

The green and white faithful roared their approval.

"Pretty soon, it became a dunk-athon," Moran said. "The place was going crazy, and the players were feeding off the crowd."

Moran was watching the spectacle with former Columbia University basketball coach Jack Rohan, who was to write a scouting report for the *New York Times* before the championship tilt.

Rob Gonzalez, who now lives in Mexico and is known as Roberto Gonzalez Narozny, was one of Michigan State's big recruits on the 1979 NCAA championship squad. *Photo courtesy of MSU Sports Information*

Rohan pointed to the tunnel where Pennsylvania was watching while waiting its turn on the floor.

"If I'm coaching, I'd get them out of there right now," Rohan said. "They don't need to see that."

Too late! The damage had already been done.

Michigan State cruised to a 50-17 halftime lead the following night en route to a 101-67 win in the NCAA semis.

"I don't know if Penn was intimidated or not, but it was never in the game," Moran said. "That's too bad, because Penn was a very good team, not your standard Ivy League team."

Moran also recalled that Michigan State and Indiana State were not the "big" stories entering the Final Four.

"All of the interest was in Penn upsetting St. John's and keeping Lou Carnesecca from reaching the Final Four, and the fact that Ray Meyer had made it to the Final Four with DePaul," Moran said.

Creating a Spartan

The night Michigan State won the NCAA championship in Salt Lake City, Mark Hollis was watching on television at home in Lexington, Michigan. He was a senior at Croswell-Lexington High School, where Lansing Waverly High School coach Phil Odlum previously graduated.

The excitement of the Spartans' win convinced Hollis he wanted to attend Michigan State. He was a football player who was injured and he wanted to stay in sports in some capacity. His high school coach set him up with an interview with MSU coach Jud Heathcote. Hollis wanted to become a team manager.

"I begged him seven times to let me come work for him for free," Hollis recalled.

In the fall of 1980, the second season after the Spartans' national title team, Hollis joined the MSU team as a manager and stayed for five years.

"My freshman year, Jud yelled at me every day. It was once a week my sophomore year and when I deserved it after that," Hollis said.

A legion of green and white followed Michigan State to the NCAA finals in Salt Lake City, Utah, and were rewarded with the Spartans' first basketball title. *Photo courtesy of MSU Sports Information*

But Hollis loved the relationship and the two are close friends today.

He currently serves Michigan State as associate athletic director for external affairs, which is a marketing job he has held since November, 1995.

Hollis has become almost nationally famous for some of his promotional ideas. He assembled the so-called "Cold War" hockey game between Michigan and Michigan State in Spartan Stadium before a world-record crowd in October, 2001—74,554 people.

Hollis also created the Coca-Cola Classic tournament field for this Thanksgiving, 2003, in the Breslin Center. The final four of 1979 will assemble as they did 25 years ago—DePaul facing Indiana State and the Spartans playing Penn with the winners playing for the championship.

"We want to make a big deal out of the 25th anniversary year," current Spartan coach Tom Izzo said. And so, he and Hollis have worked for more than a year to create a special observance for the 1979 Spartans.

A Special Visitor

Among those MSU fans in Salt Lake City for the Final Four in 1979 was none other than Tom Izzo himself. He was invited by the powerful Upper Peninsula state legislator Dominic Jacobetti. Izzo was completing his first season as an assistant coach at Northern Michigan University, his alma mater, under head coach Glenn Brown. The NMU coaches were among Jacobetti's guests.

"We had great seats," Izzo recalls. "I was always an MSU fan."

Izzo's first attendance at a coaching clinic was at Michigan State before the 1978-1979 season began.

"I went to Jud's clinic and watched him yell at Earvin and Kelser back in October of that season," Tom said. "I laughed because of how tough he was with players who were that good. I shook Jud's hand and met his assistant coaches, Edgar Wilson and Dave Harshman."

Izzo also played against Michigan State while a member of the Northern Michigan team. His first start in college was during the 1975 season. The Spartans, who won the game, traveled to Marquette under coach Gus Ganakas. It was during that season that Tom Izzo decided that one day he wanted to become a head basketball coach in college.

"Go Green"

Officials in Utah went all out to find activities for fans attending the 1979 NCAA Final Four in Salt Lake City. And in some cases, the MSU fans received extra special treatment.

A Spartan alum was in charge of skiing at the nearby Park City, Utah, resort. On the Sunday between the semifinals and championship game, numerous MSU fans skied down the beautiful Utah slopes.

All of the lift tickets sold that day were inscribed "Go Green."

It was a glorious day between games for MSU's cheerleaders, students, and fans whiling away the time before the big game the next night against unbeaten Indiana State.

Wrong Song

Rarely, if ever, does the Mormon Tabernacle Choir mess up one of its presentations. But such was the case the night before the NCAA semifinals in Salt Lake City in 1979.

All of the schools involved were invited to a special concert.

An announcer would welcome each school's fans followed, by the singing of that school's fight song by the choir. Michigan State's fans were saluted last.

The choir promptly sang a mighty rendition of "The Victors," which, of course, is the official fight song of the University of Michigan. To say the Spartan following was upset was an understatement. It was a bad way to start the weekend for the Spartan faithful, but they did smile before their trip ended the following Monday.

The Greatest Trip

Bob Steele retired this summer after 35 years of teaching at White Hills Elementary School in East Lansing.

In 1979, several years into his teaching tenure, Steele was earning "about $10,000 per year."

He was a former track star at Michigan State and a member of the Varsity Club as an alumnus. Steele loved following the MSU basketball team and he was especially in awe of Earvin "Magic" Johnson.

Steele noticed that a weekend at the Final Four in Salt Lake City was available to Varsity Club members for $600 while tickets were still available. Steele talked two friends, one of whom was former MSU track star Keith Coates, into making the trip.

"It was the greatest sports weekend I've ever enjoyed in my life," Steele recalled.

The tickets were not in the greatest location.

"Top row for the semifinals," Steele said.

The morning of the championship game, the Steele trio was eating breakfast in the hotel coffee shop with numerous MSU and Indiana State fans. The trash talking was in full force.

"They kept telling us that Kelser was the star of our team," Steele said.

"We kept telling them that America had 100 Kelsers and that Earvin was the guy who would make the difference that night."

A short time later, Steele bumped into MSU Ralph Young Fund Director Terry Braverman. The two were acquaintances from Steele's varsity days as an athlete. Braverman inquired about Steele's seat location and told him to come to his room.

On Braverman's bed were hundreds of championship game tickets soon to be distributed to various Spartan fans.

Because an MSU board of trustee member cancelled out on the trip, Braverman exchanged tickets, and Steele and his buddies sat ten rows behind the MSU team. They thought they'd died and gone to heaven that night.

The location provided a good seat from which to yell at Indiana State fans across the way.

"They kept yelling '33-0'. We yelled back, '32-1," said Steele, in reference to the final record Indiana State would have after the game ended.

In their euphoria after the game, Steele and his buddies drove their rental car to nearby Stateline, Nevada that night and headed for the nearest casino.

Steele won $280, which helped pay for his trip.

Final Interviews

A local Salt Lake City television station was airing interviews during the late newscast the night before the game between Michigan State and Indiana State. All ten starters popped up on the screen for brief comments.

In their own way, the first nine players talked about how fabulous it was to be playing in such an important game and how they just hoped they'd play well—words to those effects.

And then Earvin Johnson's face appeared. He described how he was born for the moment, that he thrived on playing in such a game and winning. Viewers said it was almost eerie how Earvin's comments were so different from the other players on each team.

Earvin expected to win and was confident the Spartans would do so. He was right, of course.

Radio Days

Several radio outlets carried the MSU basketball games at the Final Four, including the school's own station announcers, Jim Adams and Terry Braverman. They called the games to a small network of stations and the broadcasts were all sponsored by agricultural outlets, fitting for an MSU product, right?

Braverman was in his fifth year of serving as MSU's Ralph Young Fund Director, the fundraising organization for athletics at the university. His department reaped immediate rewards from the Spartans' victory over Indiana State.

Ralph Young Fund contributions jumped from $600,000 to $970,000 in the year following the Spartans' championship. That was more than a 50 percent increase. A good year nets about a seven to ten percent increase, according to Braverman. Today, by comparison, the Ralph Young Fund takes in some $9 million per year in donor contributions.

Earvin "Magic" Johnson reveled in the spotlight, often leaving the media shaking their heads with his thoughtful yet candid, honest, and sometimes humorous answers. *Photo courtesy of MSU Sports Information*

After the championship game, MSU's admissions office reported a triple jump in student applications for enrollment.

The team banquet in April drew 1,600 fans to what was then known as Long's Banquet Center (which is today the Holiday Inn South). It is still considered the largest-attended banquet in MSU sports history. It was carried live by WJIM-TV, the CBS affiliate, and hosted by co-author Tim Staudt, who also presented one of the Most Valuable Player awards.

Extra security police were hired to safeguard the banquet from outside intruders who didn't have tickets.

Braverman was involved in most MSU basketball activities in those days, and today he serves as the public address announcer at both home football and basketball games. He retired as Ralph Young Fund Director in the summer of 2002 after 38 years of employment with the university.

CHAPTER 5

The Championship Game

Reaching Final Four Not Enough

Because so few coaches ever get to take a team to the NCAA championships, Jud Heathcote once said that reaching the Final Four was as big as winning it all.

That all changed when Heathcote, the ultimate competitor, arrived in Salt Lake City.

"Once I got there, it was all about winning," he said. "After we beat Penn, the buildup for the final game with Indiana State was incredible. Heck, Indiana State was 33-0 and we were five-point favorites."

The Spartans led by nine at the half, 37-28, and scored the first seven points of the second half for a 44-28 lead with 17:22 to play.

"I think we were on the verge of blowing it open like we did against Penn [101-67 semi triumph]," Heathcote said.

However, 6'8" senior Gregory Kelser was called for a charge and had to come out with his fourth foul.

"Our 16-point lead disappeared to seven," Heathcote recalled. "I never felt comfortable until Earvin made a basket, and the Indiana State player [Bobby Heaton] was called for a flagrant foul for undercutting him.

"That call could have gone either way. I felt a little better after that one."

Magic meshed the two free throws, and the four-point play made it 61-50 with six minutes remaining. With Kelser playing the rest of the way, the Spartans and a "more relaxed" Heathcote won it 75-64.

Serious Ride

For the most part, Michigan State's basketball team was a pretty loose group on its way to arenas prior to games. There was often small talk, some singing and lots of music.

Spartans manager Randy Bishop noticed a different attitude, however, in the van ride to the Special Events Center on the campus of the University of Utah before the championship game.

"Earvin Johnson was in the van along with a couple of others, and it wasn't fun and games," Bishop said. "There was some serious thought going on. I wasn't sure if it was nerves or not.

"Looking back on all of the successes of that season, and the success Earvin had since then, I have to conclude that it was mental preparation—maybe even sensing destiny."

It may have been "destiny," but Indiana State made sure it wasn't a romp in the park.

Bishop recalled that head coach Jud Heathcote turned to assistant Dave Harshman and said, "This is tough."

To which Harshman said, "Did you think it was going to be easy?"

Bishop particularly enjoyed Gregory Kelser's "statement" slam dunk at the end of the game to make the final score, 75-64.

"My mother-in-law was in an office pool, and lost because of that basket," Bishop said. "I think she got over it."

Earvin Johnson and his wife, Cookie, with Andre, Earvin III (in the Lakers warmup), and Elisa.
Photo courtesy of the Johnson family

Gregory Lloyd and his wife, Veronica, with Whitney and Omar.
Photo courtesy of the Lloyd family

Rick Kaye lives in Milford and remains a loyal Spartan football and basketball fan, attending as many games as possible.
Photo courtesy of the Kaye family

Gerald Gilkie with his son Marcus.
Photo courtesy of the Gilkie family

Help him shoot for the stars...
(First you need life insurance.)

When you give your kids security, you give them a better shot at the future.

Make sure you have the security of permanent life insurance from Farm Bureau Life Insurance Company of Michigan.

Permanent life insurance means permanent protection, the foundation of financial security for you and your family. Call your Farm Bureau Insurance agent today.

Coauthors Tim Staudt (left) and Fred Stabley, Jr. flank Earvin Johnson during their interview at Magic's East Lansing Starbucks.
Photo courtesy of Fred Stabley, Jr.

Terry Donnelly and his wife, Melissa, with his daughter, Claire, and son, Nicholas.
Photo courtesy of the Donnelly family

Gregory Kelser and his wife, Donna, dated for 11 years before marrying in 1986.
Photo courtesy of the Kelser family

Jaimie "Shoes" Huffman now calls a 90-acre ranch south of Dallas his home.
Photo courtesy of the Huffman family

From Sick Bed to National Hero

There was never a doubt in Terry Donnelly's mind that he was going to play in the 1979 NCAA championship tilt against Indiana State.

His stomach and tailbone may have had other ideas, though.

Donnelly spent two days in bed following the semifinal romp over Pennsylvania, a game in which he hurt his tailbone when undercut on a layup.

However, it was an upset stomach that kept him bedridden.

"I had a temperature of 103 and ate only two pancakes in two days," Donnelly said. "I don't know what the problem was, but the coaches did a good job of keeping it quiet.

"It could have been nerves or a stomach virus. I was going to try and play, regardless."

The slender 6'2" lefty was the unlikely hero in the game filled with superstars when he nailed 15 points to help the Spartans win the title.

How did Donnelly celebrate the championship?

"I went back to the hotel and went to bed," he said. "I was dehydrated and dead tired."

Who Said That?

Larry Bird wasn't big on the media when he was at Indiana State.

In fact, the shy superstar would miss a press conference if he could.

But it still came as quite a surprise to Michigan State assistant sports information director Nick Vista when he saw Indiana State sports information director Ed McKee writing at a feverish pace late in the championship game in Salt Lake City.

You'd never guess by looking at this picture, but Terry Donnelly crawled out of a sick bed to help lead Michigan State to victory over Indiana State in the NCAA finals. He didn't miss a shot in five tries from the floor and finished with 15 points. *Photo courtesy of MSU Sports Information*

Vista finally asked McKee what he was doing, and he said he was writing Bird's "words" to the media because Larry would not be attending the postgame press conference.

Conversely, Vista has explicit memories of Spartan media darlings Gregory Kelser and Earvin Johnson.

"I remember at one of the press conferences when they told the media they'd be happy to spend as much time with them as desired," Vista said. "It was quite a difference between the stars of the two schools."

McKee recalled the additional media attention during Bird's senior season as the Sycamores kept winning games.

"All kinds of people were assigned to come to Terre Haute, and most of them wanted to talk with Larry," McKee said. "I could never in good conscience assure them of an interview with him.

"I could promise them an interview with one of Larry's teammates, and I was always trying to pitch our gymnastics Olympian, Kurt Thomas, to people. Very few people ever got an interview with Larry, though."

Proud Parents in Salt Lake City

W alter Kelser just couldn't help himself.

All year long, Gregory Kelser's father has resisted the urge to join in with the Michigan State faithful when they bellowed out "Kelser, Kelser, Kelser" in honor of his son.

But sitting in the Special Events Center on the campus of the University of Utah, Walter had to join the chorus, too. It was during the Spartans' 101-67 semifinal win over Pennsylvania, and Kelser had taken a seat on the bench with 28 points, nine rebounds, and four blocks to his credit.

"Normally, I'll just sit there with a warm feeling from head to toe," Walter said, laughing. "But I just couldn't help myself this time. I had to start shouting, too.

"It seemed funny yelling my own name, but I got all wrapped up in the thing."

Walter Kelser, who passed away in 1984, reveled in the championship game as well, when his son had 19 points, nine assists, and eight rebounds in the 75-64 win over Indiana State.

He found one thing more pleasing, though, and that's when his son was named academic All-American. "That was the best of all," Walter said. "That made me very proud. He's more than just a great basketball player."

Walter, who spent 20 years in the Air Force, knew his son was going to be a good basketball player at a young age. He was stationed in Okinawa when Gregory asked his dad to come and watch him play.

Gregory scored 26 points in the game, and his team won, 26-0.

"From then on, we spent a lot of time playing basketball," Walter said.

Walter and his wife, Verna, were among six sets of parents at the Final Four. Also in attendance were the parents of Terry Donnelly, Rob Gonzalez, Jaimie Huffman, Earvin Johnson, and Mike Longaker.

Christine Johnson, Magic's mother, did not see the semifinal win. She's a Seventh Day Adventist and never watched a game on Saturday. She didn't find out who won until the family returned to the hotel room.

But she was there on Monday for the championship tilt along with Earvin Sr. and a couple thousand more Spartan fans who made the cross-country trek.

Earvin's father also had an idea his son was going to be a good player at a precocious age.

"We'd watch the pro games on TV every Sunday and he was always interested in what was going on," said Earvin Sr. "Pretty soon, Earvin and his brother Larry would roll up some socks and race around the house pretending they were dunking a ball off the wall.

"He really loved the game. He used to get up early on many days and run down to Main Street School to play basketball and then get back home before it was time to go to school."

Interesting tales from proud Spartan parents.

One Last Pass

After watching Earvin Johnson for three years in high school and all 62 games of his college career, few things "Magic" did surprised me.

One thing that I did wonder about for a long time, though, was the last pass of his collegiate career in the 75-64 win over Indiana State in the 1979 NCAA championship tilt.

You may remember it as well.

With the final seconds ticking away, Earvin took the ball out of the net following an Indiana State basket, stepped out of bounds, and threw the ball over his head blindly down the floor.

Predictably, the ball hit Gregory Kelser on the dead run past halfcourt, and he raced in for a dunk to end the game.

Years later, I asked Earvin about the pass.

"When the shot went up, I saw Gregory taking off out of the corner of my eye," Magic said, with a laugh. "I just stepped out of bounds and tossed it as far as I could over my head."

Just one of school-record 269 assists that season, but a remarkable one nonetheless.

—*Fred Stabley Jr.*

Media Musings From Final Four

The media descended on the 1979 Final Four like no other collegiate basketball championship in history.

You can easily see why when two of the most celebrated players in college basketball were featured in Indiana State's Larry Bird and Michigan State's Earvin Johnson. The Spartans' Gregory Kelser and Jay Vincent and DePaul's Mark Aguirre were draws also.

MSU coach Jud Heathcote remembers a couple of incidents in Salt Lake City vividly.

"We had a press conference between the semis and the finals, and we took Earvin and Gregory," Heathcote said. "On the way over, I kept telling them to be careful because the media was going to try to get them to compare Bird and Magic, or something like that.

"When we got in the car and headed back to the hotel, Earvin and Gregory were laughing hard in the back seat."

"Those people must have thought we were nuts," one of them said. "All we did was praise Larry Bird the whole press conference."

The Spartans did a great job keeping Indiana State's Larry Bird (right) in check during MSU's 75-64 NCAA championship final. One of the reasons was the play of senior Gregory Kelser. *Photo courtesy of MSU Sports Information*

A day later, after the Spartan victory, Heathcote took his five starters to the postgame interview, where they were grilled for 45 minutes.

Finally, there was one writer left and he kept on trying to get the MSU players to say something bad about Bird by saying: "He let his team down; what did you think of his play?"

Jud had heard enough and told the freelance writer, "If you ask one more question like that, I'll throw you out of this room myself."

Heathcote then added: "Just put down that Larry Bird and Earvin Johnson will be two of the greatest players in NBA history. They have vision and great hands."

MSU Fans No. 1, Too

Michigan State's fan following in 1979 was almost as incredible as the Spartan basketball team itself.

I still get goose bumps thinking about the legions of green and white that made the trips to Indianapolis for the regional finals and to Salt Lake City for the finals, never passing up the opportunity to let strangers know who they were rooting for.

You would hear the Spartan Fight Song burst out all over the downtown areas of those relatively conservative cities.

Just four hours from MSU, Indianapolis became East Lansing South. The pregame hype started in the wee hours of Sunday, March 18, with crescendos of the fight song echoing throughout the city. The uproar became more intense with a pep rally at the War Memorial in Monument Circle and reached a fevered pitch in a parade of Spartan loyalists that blocked traffic en route to Market Square Arena.

The enthusiasm and electricity was transmitted to the MSU team as it pounded out an 80-68 win over Notre Dame to reach the Final Four for the first time since 1957.

The numbers weren't quite the same in Salt Lake City because of distance, but the Spartan fans were just as noisy and supportive.

Michigan State clobbered Pennsylvania, 101-67, in the semis, and near the end of the game the Spartan fans started a rhythmic chant: "We want the Bird! We want the Bird! We want the Bird!" Even before Indiana State sidelined Mark Aguirre and DePaul in the other semi thriller, 76-74, the Sycamore fans were answering with "You'll get the Bird!"

Just as MSU fans did before the regional finals, they held a massive pep rally in downtown Salt Lake City and passed out "bird stuffing" (the kind used on a Thanksgiving turkey). Led by the band and cheerleaders, they marched around Temple Square, where the famous Mormon Tabernacle choir performed, and sang the fight song at least a dozen times.

After the 75-64 victory, the celebration began from coast to coast for MSU fans, most notably in East Lansing. "It sounded like World War III had started," a person who lived less than one-half mile from campus said.

For the fans in Salt Lake City, who did plenty of celebrating themselves, their only regret was that they weren't back in East Lansing to join in the fun there.

—*Fred Stabley Jr.*

No Time to Celebrate

L ynn Henning and I covered the 1979 NCAA basketball finals for *The State Journal*, Lansing's daily paper, in Salt Lake City, Utah.

Lynn, who has gone on to bigger and better things in the newspaper world with *The Detroit News*, was the columnist and I was the beat reporter.

While two seemed plenty back in 1979, to show you how times have changed, *The State Journal* assigned four people to cover the Spartans' 2000 championship in Indianapolis.

Nevertheless, it was Lynn and me … a two-man fast break, so to speak.

When the championship game was over and the Spartans were victorious, our evening was just beginning. *The State Journal* was an afternoon paper then, so we had no deadlines to meet, and we spent every second possible talking with the players, coaches and fans for stories in the Tuesday, March 27, edition.

I was accused by some of my friends (watching on TV back in Michigan) of joining the MSU fans on the floor and celebrating the championship—something I undoubtedly would have done if I weren't working. I was on the floor as the designated pool reporter to grab a couple of quick quotes from head coach Jud Heathcote to give to the reporters on deadline.

Lynn and I spent the next three hours or so banging out stories in a makeshift press room a couple of hundred yards from the Special Events Center. Lynn wrote a color piece for page one of the newspaper, a column and a sidebar while I wrote the game story for the sports page and three sidebars on Earvin Johnson, Gregory Kelser and Terry Donnelly.

It was sometime between two and three in the morning when we had filed our stories and left the press room. We walked out into the cool Utah air, directly facing the snow-peaked Wasatch Mountain range.

Almost spontaneously we hollered out to no one but ourselves … "NCAA champions!"

Hey, a couple of Spartan grads, even reporters, are allowed at least one cheer.

—*Fred Stabley Jr.*

Welcome Home!

Everyone has a memory of MSU's NCAA basketball championship in 1979.

For me, it was quite simple.

The welcome home to Jenison Field House on the day after winning the title was the most emotional event I'd ever been a part of, and I'm a pretty emotional guy.

With more than 10,000 people jammed into the "old barn," the Spartan heroes were greeted and feted one more time. The roof of Jenison was raised again, and there were few dry eyes in the place. I know mine weren't.

The din was deafening when MSU's players made their way to a make-shift stage at midcourt.

"We had a tremendous time in Utah and wish all of you could have been there to share our success," Gregory Kelser said. "But I'm sure you saw it on TV and just like long distance, it's the next best thing to being there."

The crowd began shouting, "Two more years ... two more years," hoping to encourage Magic Johnson to return to Michigan State.

"Wow!!! Oh man!!! We went to Utah with a job to do and we did it," Magic said. "We want you to know we've got the No. 1 cheerleaders, the No. 1 team and you are the No. 1 fans."

Nobody wanted it to end, and the cheering didn't for a long time. It was an exceptionally special moment for me.

—*Fred Stabley Jr.*

* P.S. I'd like to give special thanks to the quick-thinking man who saw my wife's dilemma when the doors opened before the ceremony. She was trying to usher three young kids into the building, and the crush of people was too much. The kindly gentleman picked up my son, Kyle, and carried him to safety past the wave of exuberant fans.

The Return Home

I did not attend the Final Four in Salt Lake City in 1979—in those days local television stations did not transmit stories from a remote location back home as easily as it is done today. My station, WJIM-TV, was a CBS affiliate. In 1979, the NCAA championship game was carried by NBC. Do any of you remember that Bryant Gumbel was a sports host in those days and interviewed the winning Spartans on the floor after the game?

After a long session of postgame interviews, the Spartans were too tired to do much else after the game and most simply went back to the hotel and went to bed. Unlike today's teams who charter almost everywhere, the '79 Spartans flew home from Salt Lake City by commercial jet the next day, making a stop along the way.

But the hometown fans were ready to party. The team arrived in Jenison Fieldhouse at about 6 p.m., where a reception was held and my television station carried all of the festivities live. Most everyone involved with the team said something from the stage located in the middle of the arena.

A parade had been planned several days before the Final Four even began that would honor the Spartans and other local teams. It was called the "Parade of Champions," and numerous civic leaders helped get all of the details worked out in short order.

On a cold March day, the parade began on Michigan Avenue and proceeded west from the Frandor Shopping Center to the State Capitol. There a reception was held for the players inside. Small cars were used, and Earvin Johnson and Greg Kelser rode in the anchor car at the back of the procession.

By the time the entourage had made it downtown, there was such bedlam I didn't think those two would survive. They were escorted through walls of people to the capitol steps, no easy task. I've always felt the Spartans had an easier time driving through opponents during the season than finding room to move through the parade route.

A short time later, the team banquet was held at the Holiday Inn South where Michigan State banquets are still held today. This event jammed more than 1,300 people inside and my station televised the festivities that night after dinner was served. I was on the program and explained to the viewing audience what all the trophies represented from the long and successful season. I presented the media's version of the Most Valuable Player award shared by both Earvin and Jay Vincent.

"We love you both," I said to the crowd, "for all of the happiness you've brought to so many people's lives."

—*Tim Staudt*

Thousands of Spartan well-wishers lined both sides of Michigan Avenue to pay tribute to the 1979 NCAA basketball champions. The parade started at Frandor Shopping Center and ended at the state capitol building. *Photo courtesy of MSU Sports Information*

The Spartans "Shut Down the City"

It was a cold and rainy day late in March of 1979—March 28, to be exact—when the Spartans made their triumphant last march down Michigan Avenue to the steps of the capitol building in Lansing as NCAA champions.

"I could not believe all of the people who lined the streets in that weather to congratulate us," said reserve guard Greg Lloyd who prepped at Lansing Eastern High, not much more than a block from the parade route.

"There were people from the campus all the way to downtown. It was amazing."

Lloyd also recalled the trip back from the airport on the Tuesday after the championship game.

"I think we shut the city down for a couple of days," he said. "We had four or five fire engines and a police escort taking us from the airport to Jenison.

"And when we pulled into Jenison, the building was full and there were people all over the parking lot, as well. None of us could believe it. The fans were incredible."

How About $50?

The final basket of Gregory Kelser's career at Michigan State came in the waning moments of the Spartans' 75-64 NCAA championship victory over Indiana State.

When a long shot from a Sycamore player went up, Earvin Johnson hollered, "Go, Greg, Go."

The lithe MSU forward took off, and the Magic Man hit him in full stride near midcourt. Kelser finished it off with a cradled whirly-bird dunk.

"I didn't think any more about it until I got a letter back at Michigan State from a guy who accused me of pouring salt in

Indiana State's wounds with the dunk," Kelser said. "He went on to say that he'd like me to send him $50 because he had given 10 points in a bet, and that dunk made the final margin 11."

Nice try ... no $50.

CHAPTER 6

Opponents

The Forgotten Miracle

One of the biggest stories from the 1979 NCAA Final Four has been virtually forgotten in the wake of the titanic showdown between the Earvin Johnson-led Spartans of Michigan State and the Larry Bird-led Sycamores of Indiana State.

That was the fact that the University of Pennsylvania had slugged its way through the East Regional to reach the pinnacle of college basketball. It was an Ivy League school fielding a powerful team without the benefit of athletic scholarships.

Bob Weinhauer hasn't forgotten, though. He was the coach of the Quakers.

"Michigan State defeated us badly in the semis, but it never diminished the fact that an Ivy League school had reached the Final Four," said Weinhauer from his retirement home at The Landings on Skidway Island near Savannah, Georgia.

"We were a lot better team than the final score, but we were not a better team than Michigan State."

The Spartans won the semifinal clash going away, 101-67, which was somewhat surprising when you consider Penn had defeated Iona (with future NBA center Jeff Ruland), North

Carolina (ranked third in the country), Syracuse and St. John's in the East Regional.

"There was no such thing as ESPN in those days, and we had never seen Michigan State play a game live," Weinhauer said. "We had one or two films to go by, none from a Big Ten team, and that was it."

One of the films was a 71-70 North Carolina win over the Spartans in Chapel Hill earlier that year.

"Based on the fact that North Carolina had beaten Michigan State, and we beat North Carolina in the tournament, we felt we could be in the game," Weinhauer said.

It was 50-17 and over at the half.

"We just didn't realize how long they were, and how quick off the floor they were," Weinhauer said. "I can remember those five starters from Michigan State like it was yesterday.

"That team had so much confidence and was at the top of its game. It was way too good inside for us on both ends of the floor. We penetrated some but didn't score, and then we lost our confidence."

Johnson had a triple-double with 29 points, 10 assists and 10 rebounds against the Quakers, something Weinhauer jokingly takes pride in.

"The next year he scored 40-something in the NBA championship game against the Philadelphia 76ers," he said. "So I guess we didn't do such a bad job against him afterall."

Gregory Kelser chipped in with 28 points, nine rebounds and four blocks, prompting Weinhauer to say in a postgame interview: "Johnson and Kelser are two of the most outstanding, dominating basketball players I have ever come across in my coaching career."

Weinhauer, who left Penn in 1982 for a three-year stint as head coach at Arizona State, spent from 1985-99 in the NBA working with Philadelphia, Atlanta, Minnesota, Houston and Milwaukee.

Still, the 1978-79 Quaker team remains special to Weinhauer, and vice versa.

When he was inducted into Philadelphia's Big Five "Hall of Fame" in January of 2002, all five of his starters returned for the ceremony.

Not Yet a TV Idol

Television exposure was much more limited in 1979, and teams like Indiana State rarely got on national telecasts. In fact, the Sycamores' first national TV game that year wasn't until their final regular-season game against Wichita State.

"We were on regional TV a lot, but the Wichita State game was our first national game," ISU interim coach Bill Hodges remembered. "A lot of people throughout the country thought that Larry Bird was black until that game."

Hodges is amazed at how college basketball has grown, and his 1978-79 Indiana State team had a major part in it.

"The number of people who watched that championship game was incredible, and I think it helped vault college basketball even more into the national spotlight," Hodges said.

It was a mixed bag, however, when Hodges looks back on it.

"We sold out every game in Larry's junior and senior season," he said. "Now there are so many games on TV that I think there's a decline in overall attendance. It's almost too saturated with college basketball games on TV now."

Two Major Events
Change Coach's Life

Two major events affected Bill Hodges's seven-year stay at Indiana State.

In his fourth year as an assistant for the Sycamores, Hodges was preparing for the start of practice in the fall of 1978 when head coach Bob King suffered a heart attack.

So on Oct. 14, Hodges became the interim head coach—one day before ISU opened drills.

He went on to lead Indiana State to 33 straight wins before falling in the NCAA championship tilt to Michigan State.

"Funny thing about that season is that it caught almost everyone by surprise," Hodges recalled. "The prognosticators picked us in the middle of the pack in the Missouri Valley. But we had the great player in Larry Bird and tremendous team chemistry."

Hodges did not have the same success, however, in subsequent years. In fact, he likened it a little to Jud Heathcote.

"We both had similar luck after that game, but Jud's president [Cecil Mackey] stuck with him and he turned it around," Hodges said. "I think we were on the verge of doing the same thing, but I didn't have the same support."

While Heathcote had three straight losing seasons before going 17-13 in 1982-83, Hodges was 16-11 in 1979-80 and then stumbled the next two.

Indiana State did manage to lure a huge recruit away from Indiana University in 6'8" Kevin Thompson from Terre Haute South High late in his tenure with the Sycamores. However, a broken rib that would not heal led to the discovery of cancer.

Thompson died on Jan. 20, 1982, and Hodges resigned on Jan. 21.

"I had some great times there, but it just didn't work out," Hodges said.

Indiana State Makes the Most of Questionable Year

Michigan State entered the 1978-79 basketball season with monstrous expectations.

Anything less than a trip to the Final Four and a strong run at an NCAA championship would have been considered disappointing.

Heck, the Spartans returned four starters from a team that lost by three (52-49) in the third round of the 1978 tournament to the eventual national champions, Kentucky, and they had Earvin Johnson—one of the top players in all of basketball.

Indiana State returned one starter—a quiet 6'9" kid from French Lick, Ind. named Larry Bird.

Very little was expected outside of the Sycamores.

To make matters worse, head coach Bob King had to step down prior to the start of the season for health reasons, leaving the job to his assistant, Bill Hodges.

A funny thing happened to the Sycamores, though. Bird put ISU on his shoulders, and it started winning and winning and never stopped until the last game of the season, when it ran into a brick wall in the form of Michigan State in the NCAA title tilt.

"Two things happened early in that year that made believers out of the players and followers alike," said former ISU sports information director Ed McKee.

One was a win over the Russian National team in the preseason (the same team Michigan State gained so much confidence from in defeating). Two was a convincing victory at Purdue.

"All of a sudden people started taking notice," McKee said. "We started having someone from the Indianapolis paper cover us on a regular basis, which was a first."

Indiana State raced through the tough Missouri Valley undefeated, although it took a last-second shot from halfcourt by Bob Heaton to force overtime in a victory at New Mexico State.

That shot was a prelude of what was to come from the "Miracle Man."

Heaton nailed last-second shots to defeat Arkansas in the regional finals and oust DePaul in the NCAA semis.

Bird took the loss to Michigan State personally.

"He was so crushed when the game ended that he put a towel over his head and just cried," McKee said. "He felt he had let his teammates, Indiana State and the whole state of Indiana down.

"He wouldn't go to the postgame press conference. He just stayed in the training room."

Most young people are resilient, and Bird didn't stay down long.

"We had a postgame celebration after the game," McKee said. "Even though we lost, we had accomplished so much that season. And when Larry showed up, his mood had changed 180 degrees."

A tired Indiana State team made its way back to Terre Haute the following day, expecting only a few diehard fans waiting for them.

"The outpouring of affection on the return was incredible," McKee said. "It seemed like there were twice as many people there when we returned then when we left. It was quite gratifying."

Who said you can't have two winners?

CHAPTER 7

Where Are They Now?

Another Brkovich Success Story

Mike Brkovich is not the only basketball-playing member of his family who has struck it rich in the private sector. Baby brother Don has built a flourishing business in Las Vegas, Nevada since opening the Don Brkovich Insurance Agency in 1992.

"We're not big, but we've been highly successful," said Brkovich of his agency just east of the Strip on Sahara Boulevard. "This area continues to grow at such an incredible rate, and everybody needs insurance."

When Brkovich moved to Las Vegas in 1990, the city had 700,000 people. By 2002, there were more than 1.5 million people.

After graduating from the University of New Mexico in 1983 with a double degree in organizational communications and management, Don worked in sales in Albuquerque until 1990.

"I was heading to San Diego," Brkovich recalled, with a chuckle. "I was 30 years old and tired of living in Albuquerque. I liked San Diego when New Mexico played basketball there.

"My plans called for me to kick back in Las Vegas for a couple of months before heading off to San Diego. I never left. It was such a booming town, and for a single guy it was fascinating."

Brkovich worked in sales for Motorola for two years while taking night classes to get his insurance license.

"Las Vegas is my home now and I'm sure this is where I'll stay," he said.

A bachelor like his older brother—"I think we're married to our careers"—Don likes to work out and travel in his spare time.

Timing Is Everything

A little gray crowding his temples and a tad more confidence in his voice are about the only differences I noticed in Mike Brkovich when we got together in one of his office buildings in Windsor.

He was still the polite, sensitive, and friendly young man that I remembered showing up at Michigan State in the fall of 1977.

"Timing is so critical in life," said a fit 6'4" Brkovich.

Timing as in being "discovered" by MSU's Jud Heathcote when the Spartans still had a scholarship left ... timing as in joining a basketball team with three superstars that would win a national championship in two years ... timing as in leaving teaching to join huge Spartan booster Richard Faber in the auto leasing business.

"I have been very fortunate in a lot of aspects of my life," Brkovich said. "I've been at the right place at the right time. I had good parents and good coaches and an outstanding business mentor."

To say that Mike is doing well for himself would be a major understatement.

He spent one year as a graduate assistant for MSU following graduation in 1981 and then got a teaching certificate at the University of Windsor. He then taught for a year in Windsor.

"Both coaching and teaching were great experiences, but they weren't for me," Brkovich recalled.

He joined Faber, owner of Fables Restaurant in Grand Rapids among his many enterprises, in 1984. Brkovich worked for Faber until 1989 when he moved back to his hometown of Windsor and started out on his own.

By the early 2000s, Brkovich owned four apartment buildings, three office buildings and three warehouses. He also owned a glass company and was in the auto exporting business.

"A lot of people don't know that I'm into auto exporting, but it's been a lucrative business for quite a while now," Brkovich said. "That's where I got the money to buy the buildings I own."

Brkovich hopes to turn two of his warehouses, once owned by Hiram Walker Whiskey, into a pair of 50-unit loft condominiums. Currently, they hold Mike's collection of more than 20 mint automobiles.

He claims no key to success other than timing and hard work.

"I'm still a conservative type of person with immigrant parents who always worked hard," Brkovich said. His mother, Mary, still lives in Windsor, while his father, Steve, passed away in 1986.

Brkovich, who owns an old home in downtown Windsor, is the perfect example of returning to his roots. He doesn't just live in Windsor but attends the same Serbian Orthodox Church he did as a child and plays basketball at the same YMCA where he learned the game nearly 30 years ago.

"I'd love to play more basketball, but my knee won't let me," Brkovich said. "I hurt my left knee in my sophomore season at Michigan State and had it scoped. I've had four more surgeries on it since."

Brkovich is active in a couple of non-profit groups and sponsors a youth basketball team. "My buddy coaches the team; I just buy the uniforms and Detroit Pistons tickets," he laughed. "It's been a lot of fun."

Through it all, Brkovich has remained single.

"I've come close a couple of times, but it just hasn't worked out," said Brkovich, who will turn 46 on April 6, 2004.

That may be the only area where Brkovich's timing has been off.

—Fred Stabley Jr.

Inside Atlanta Federal Prison: Ron Charles

When Ron "Bobo" Charles's professional basketball career came to an end in 1988, he had to find a place to call home.

He liked big cities. He liked it warm. He picked Atlanta.

Charles filled out a number of job applications and got a job in 1989 at the Atlanta Federal Prison as a recreation specialist.

Much to his surprise, he's still there.

"It's a good job, and you do meet some interesting people," Charles explained. "I never figured I'd be working there that long, but I'll have 20 years in by 2009 and I can retire.

"We have a lot of lifers in here and some pretty good athletes. I just supervise the recreation programs and make sure there are no fights. That's a job in itself."

The Rev. Jim Bakker and former Kansas City Royals rookie standout Willie Mays Aikens are among those who have been inside the Atlanta prison in Bobo's tenure, although Bakker did not take part in recreational activities.

After graduating with a degree in elementary education in 1980, Charles was drafted by the NBA's Chicago Bulls but did not make it. He went back to MSU, took graduate classes and coached the junior varsity.

He then launched a professional career of nearly eight years that took him to Spain, France, Italy, Switzerland, Sweden, Argentina and Chile. He once ran into Sten Feldreich, a seven-footer from Sweden who played for Michigan State in 1977-78.

"He was a big-time TV and newspaperman there," Charles said. "His pro career was over and we had some nice visits."

The 6'8" Charles injured his ankle so badly while playing in Chile in 1988 that it took two years for it to heal.

"That ended my playing career, although I still play a little now," said Charles, who lives in Riverdale, a suburb south of Atlanta.

He and his second wife, Melodia, are the parents of a son, Jaron (born 4-5-01). Ron has another son from his first marriage, Ronald (born 11-2-92), who lives in Chicago.

Bobo will turn 45 on Jan. 23 (2004). He has coached a recreation team of 10 and 11 year olds since 1997, and loves it.

Is he tough on them?

"That's not my style," Charles laughed. "I let them play … let them have fun."

It's a Small World After All

It was shortly after Terry Donnelly had moved from Houston to Dallas that he was eating lunch at a Chick-Fil-A and a familiar face walked into the restaurant.

"I couldn't believe it, but there was an old buddy of mine from Michigan State, Rod Strata," Donnelly said of the former Spartan football standout. "We hadn't seen each other in almost 10 years. The last I knew he was in Nashville when I was living in Atlanta.

"We both kidded each other about how much hair we had lost."

They now live four miles apart from each other and get together at least two or three times a month to play golf.

Other than his four-year stay in East Lansing, Donnelly has always seemed to live in big towns. He came to MSU from St. Louis and graduated in 1980 with a degree in business administration.

Donnelly went to Atlanta, where he worked as a stockbroker until heading to Houston in 1990 to join the family business— a paper converter and ribbon manufacturing company.

Terry was single until 1996 when he married Melissa, an executive with National Cash Register. She was transferred to Dallas, and the family moved there in 2000.

"I work out of my house in Dallas and handle the sales operations for my company," Donnelly said. "We were regional when we started, but now we're nationwide."

The Donnelly family now consists of Claire Nicole (born 11-9-98) and Nicholas Christian (born 6-15-02).

"We had our family late and that's it as far as I'm concerned," said Donnelly, who turned 45 on August 28, 2003.

A Tennis Ace

When Terry Donnelly grew up in St. Louis, Missouri, he spent much of his time with a basketball or a set of golf clubs in his hands.

However, the former standout guard at Michigan State found he had skills in another sport when he moved to Atlanta following college.

"Atlanta is like the tennis capital of the world," Donnelly said. "Everybody played tennis or ran, and I did both."

Donnelly ran in a number of 10Ks but found he accomplished more with a tennis racket in his hand.

When he moved to Houston in 1990, Donnelly and his partner were ranked No. 1 in doubles in the Texas Section and had a 4.5 rating from the United States Tennis Association. They won a number of zone tourneys and were 23-0 one year.

"I played a lot until I was 36 years old and got married," Donnelly said. "Now I play once a week in a league."

Donnelly still enjoys playing golf, where he carries a single-digit handicap.

A Future Spartan?

When little Marcus Dean Gilkie sees the Intramural Building on the campus of Michigan State University, he gets excited and starts hollering, "Ball ... ball."

The son of former Spartan Gerald Gilkie, Marcus Dean (born in November of 2000) already has an eye on the game of basketball.

"I get a kick out of taking him with me to play basketball," Gilkie said.

Marcus Dean will have a good coach as he grows up.

Father Gerald was a member of MSU's 1979 NCAA championship team and kept his hand in basketball for many years after while working at Camp Highfields from 1982-95. His primary job was as a residential counselor at the facility for delinquent boys. He also coached its basketball team.

"We usually played facilities like ours," Gilkie said. "However, once we played Lansing Everett's junior varsity and got spanked pretty good."

The coach for Everett was Gilkie's roommate and former Spartan teammate, Jaimie "Shoes" Huffman.

A criminal justice major at Michigan State, the Detroit Kettering High product went to the Ionia State Prison in 1995 as an officer and became a counselor in 1998—a position he still holds.

Gilkie, who lives in Lansing and makes a 45-minute commute to work, enjoys playing golf and lifting weights in his spare time. He also likes more cultural endeavors like going to concerts and plays.

And taking Marcus Dean to play basketball.

Dual Citizenship

When he left Michigan State, he was Rob Gonzalez. Now, he's Roberto Gonzalez Narozny of Mexico City, Mexico.

"My given name was Roberto from my father's Mexican heritage, and my mother's maiden name is Narozny," he explained. "In Mexico, you use your mother's maiden name on official documents."

After finishing his college career at the University of Colorado, Gonzalez kept his hand in basketball by playing for the Mexican National team.

He's been in Mexico since 1988, first as a player, then as a representative of the Mexican Basketball Federation and now as the owner of a sports marketing firm and promotional company that is helping to develop basketball in the country.

One of the players he represents is Eduardo Najera (University of Oklahoma), who has been a member of the Dallas Mavericks for the past two seasons.

You may remember Najera as the player who had the violent collision with Michigan State's Mateen Cleaves in an NCAA regional game in 1999.

Gonzalez married a Mexican woman, Beatriz Juarez, and they have one son, Roberto Jr. (June of 2001).

"I don't play basketball competitively any more, although I will shoot around with friends," he said.

Rob remains friends with Earvin Johnson, who has been to Mexico on six different occasions to help support the fledgling basketball programs there. He also served on a board of directors with the President of Mexico (Vincente Fox) to help support and raise income for areas of the country that have been devastated by immigration and poverty.

In his spare time, Gonzalez enjoys traveling in Mexico and following college basketball.

A Tall Texan

He owns a 90-acre ranch some 30 miles south of Dallas. He has season tickets to the Dallas Mavericks.

He's a middleman in a tire recycling company.

And he's a strong Christian who tries to make a difference each day.

Meet Jaimie Huffman, 25 years after throwing a shoe and becoming famous when the late Al McGuire dubbed him "Shoes" Huffman during Michigan State's NCAA regional tilt with Lamar.

Huffman came to the Lone Star state in 1985, where he built a successful check certifying company and sold it. He was married for 10 years before getting divorced.

However, it was his former wife (still a good friend) who led him to church and a Christian life.

"I'm motivated by being positive and constructive each day," said Huffman, who was born on May 8, 1958. "I want to be a good example for others."

Huffman is now a volunteer for Habitat for Humanity and is a facilitator for a divorce group at his church that helped him through some tough times.

"It's a matter of giving back," Huffman said. "I went through it and now I want to help others."

Huffman has longhorn cattle on his ranch along with some Arabian horses and a border collie. "I love animals," he said. "The longhorns can walk right up and look at you through the window."

He hasn't lost his love for sports, either, and basketball in particular.

"I have tickets about three rows behind Mavericks owner Mark Cuban," Huffman said. "It's the best seat in the house. All of the teams run right by me. The only bad thing is that Cuban is on his feet so much that he blocks your vision."

The one thing that Huffman would like to do in future years is travel.

"There's so much out there I haven't seen," he said. "I plan on traveling a lot."

Finished Career
at Ferris State

After seeing the handwriting on the wall—that is, lack of playing time—Jaimie Huffman left Michigan State and transferred to Ferris State.

"I wanted to play, but I wasn't all that smart," Huffman said, chuckling. "I helped recruit a couple of guards to go to Ferris, including Dale Beard from Lansing Everett. So we ended up with five or six good guards, and my playing time was limited.

"It was then I decided I'd better get on with my life, graduate and find something to do with my life."

After graduating from Ferris State with a degree in business administration, Huffman moved back to East Lansing, where he went to school to get a master's degree in hotel and restaurant administration. He coached the freshman boys and junior varsity girls at his alma mater, Everett, for three years.

"I enjoyed coaching and sometimes wish I had stayed with it," Huffman said.

He might have had it not been for a "hairnet."

"I was working in Wonders Hall at Michigan State as an assistant food manager," Huffman said. "I was asked to wear a hairnet even though I never handled the food. So many of the Spartans athletes ate there and they were my friends.

"Looking back, I should have done it, but I didn't want to. I was going to be written up for insubordination, and I told them to save the time that I was going to quit."

Huffman loaded his Camaro with all of his worldly possessions, left Michigan and his coaching ambitions behind, and headed for Texas.

A Trip Down Memory Lane

J aimie Huffman relived Michigan State's NCAA championship in March of 2002 by following Kent State's trip to the Elite Eight.

You may recall that the catalyst for the Golden Flashes was a 6'1" senior guard from Petoskey, Mich., named Trevor Huffman—Jaimie's nephew.

"I went all over the country watching him play," Jaimie said. "It was great. He's a heckuva player and it was a thrill watching Kent play."

Jaimie drove from his home in the Dallas area to NCAA tourney games in Lexington, Ky., and Greenville, S.C.

Incidentally, Trevor Huffman had another Spartan tie while playing for Kent State—his first-year coach was Stan Heath, fresh off Tom Izzo's staff at Michigan State.

"Storybook Life"

T humbing through a copy of *Sports Illustrated* last December, there was a picture of Earvin "Magic" Johnson.

That's not noteworthy, in itself, as few athletes in history have been featured on the cover or inside the magazine as much as Magic.

However, this one didn't praise Earvin for his basketball prowess or talk about his successes in the world of business. Far from it.

In small print in the upper left-hand corner of the full page ad read, "Diagnosed with HIV in 1991." Below a big picture of Magic with his eyes closed and fists clenched was a statement from Earvin: "HIV changed my life, but it doesn't keep me from living."

It's not a reach to call Magic the "poster child" for HIV, the virus that leads to AIDS. Earvin is proof that you not only can live with HIV ... but flourish.

Then again, hasn't that been the case throughout his "storybook life?"

"I've been blessed with three lives ... basketball, business, and HIV," Earvin said. "I was able to excel in basketball, and I've had more success in business than I ever thought.

"And then I wear the badge of HIV with honor. I want to bring an awareness of HIV to young people everywhere. I wouldn't change anything in my life."

With good reason!

Magic has had the "Midas touch" in everything he's done.

First, in a matter of a mere four years, Earvin was on teams that won a state high school title, an NCAA championship, and an NBA crown. His teams proceeded to win five NBA titles, and he culminated his playing career with a gold medal in the 1996 Olympics. He was inducted into the Basketball Hall of Fame in September of 2002.

Second, he's an exceptionally successful businessman, serving as the CEO of Magic Johnson Enterprises. He employs more than 3,000 people nationwide and is worth countless millions.

Third, it will be 12 years in October of 2003 that he's lived with HIV, defying the odds as he's done his entire life. Earvin tackles every challenge with lifelong traits—hard work and a smile.

"I get my work ethic from my dad [Earvin Sr.], who is my role model," he said. "And I get my personality from my mother [Christine]."

It's been an incredible combination.

Magic will also tell you that wife Cookie and he have also been a fabulous combination since their marriage in 1991.

They live in Beverly Hills and have two children—Earvin III (born 6-4-92) and Elisa (12-21-94). Magic also has another son, Andre (2-6-81).

Cookie, who works out every morning like Magic does, is on the board of directors for the Magic Johnson Foundation, and is also involved in breast cancer awareness.

"Haven't Missed a Beat"

It was at Michigan State's 20-year reunion party, and the jokes and stories were flying around the room when Jeanne Kaye turned to her husband, Rick, and said, "You guys haven't missed a beat in 20 years."

The camaraderie and oneness, key elements in the Spartans' title season, were still evident two decades later.

"We knew we had the potential to win it all after losing such a close game to Kentucky (52-49) in the regional finals the previous season," Kaye said. "We had a group of guys come together with the goals of winning the Big Ten and NCAA titles.

"We worked hard, and everyone got along so well."

The thought of playing with Earvin Johnson at MSU was one of the reasons Kaye chose the Spartans after an outstanding career at Detroit Catholic Central.

"Michigan State and Vern Payne had been recruiting me all season," the 6'7" forward said. "I came up for my official visit and had a good weekend.

"Jud [Heathcote] gave me a couple of days to think about it, but my mind was pretty well made up. Plus, the feeling from coach Payne was that Earvin was going to come to MSU, and that would be a bonus."

While Earvin did opt for the green and white, Kaye's playing time was limited in his first two seasons when the Spartans went 51-11 and won two Big Ten titles. However, he saw more action as a junior and was a starter in his senior season.

Kaye did play seven minutes in the NCAA semifinal romp of Pennsylvania and scored five points, had two rebounds and an assist.

"I was on the receiving end of that behind-the-back pass from [Jaimie] Huffman," Kaye said. "We all got a lot of playing time in that game, which made it special."

Kaye wisely divided his time in East Lansing between the classroom and basketball floor.

"I was there for an education, and I took advantage of it," Kaye said. "I knew my chances of making it in the NBA were not very good, so I made sure I took care of my academics."

Kaye graduated from MSU in 1982 with a dual major in packaging and engineering.

His first job out of college was working as a distributing and warehousing supervisor for Vernor's in Detroit from 1982-84. Rick then spent from 1984-88 as a district manager for Crain Communications as the distribution manager for magazines.

Kaye got a job at Chrysler in 1988 and has been there ever since. His latest position with DaimlerChrysler was as a project manager for powertrain platforms.

Rick and his wife live in Milford and have three daughters— Cara, Jillian, and Erin.

Kaye (born 3-14-59) still plays basketball in pickup games, and loves golf, where he has lowered his handicap to 12.

And he still enjoys going to Spartan football and basketball games.

Perfectionism

Gregory Kelser feels fortunate to have played for Jud Heathcote.

"There's no question he made me a better basketball player," Kelser said. "I consider Jud a friend and a positive influence in my life.

"He strove for perfection. He always taught me to work beyond 'good enough.' He was difficult to play for. Would I do it again? Absolutely! I didn't understand it when going through it, but he helped mold me as a person."

Heathcote's influence can be felt still on the personable All-American, who is in the midst of a successful career in radio and television that followed six years in the NBA.

"I'm big on preparation for games, and I think that comes from Jud," Kelser said. "I spend a lot of time doing my homework out of my office at home."

Kelser was the first-round draft choice of the Detroit Pistons in 1979, fourth overall, and spent two years in the Motor City before going to Seattle for two years. He then went to the Los Angeles Clippers for a year before finishing his career with the Indianapolis Pacers.

"I began to have knee problems in my second year and had tendinitis in both knees," Kelser said. "I had four solid years, but after that I never got back to 100 percent."

Still, Kelser was hoping to sign an NBA contract in 1985, willing to endure the pain if the price were right.

The only contract offer came from the Cleveland Cavaliers, and it wasn't one Kelser considered "fair."

So the well-spoken 1981 MSU graduate with a degree in social science turned his sneakers in for a microphone.

Kelser got his "start" in friend Charlie Neal's house.

"We'd put a basketball tape in his VCR and do a mock broadcast," Kelser recalled.

Neal eventually hired Kelser to do color commentary for the Black Entertainment Network that telecast black schools' basketball games throughout the South.

Although Kelser kept his BET gig for six years until 1992, he began doing Big Ten basketball games in 1987. He worked on the Pistons radio network from 1988-93 and moved to the Pistons TV network in 1993. He also worked on the Minnesota Timberwolves TV network from 1991-95.

Kelser has had his share of national exposure in recent years, working with Fox and ESPN. He's worked for CBS in its coverage of NCAA regional basketball the past six seasons.

"We work six games in two days for CBS," Kelser said. "It's busy, but I love it."

It gives him a taste of what he'd like to do on a more regular basis.

"I would love more consistent work on a national scope," Kelser said. "That's what I'm working for."

Kelser will be the first to tell you that life has been good.

"I feel fortunate and blessed," he said.

In addition to doing more than 90 basketball game a year (he also does WNBA and high school state final games), Gregory runs two basketball camps in Southfield and is a motivational speaker.

Kelser and his wife, Donna, recently designed their new 4,000-foot home in Franklin Hills, where Gregory enjoys his quiet time by reading and listening to jazz.

Donna and Gregory dated for 11 years before marrying in 1986, and they have no children.

They both travel a lot in their jobs—Gregory doing basketball games and Donna as a flight attendant for Northwest Airlines. She also owns a hair salon in Southfield and works part-time for Paul Mitchell as a designer.

Kelser (born Sept. 17, 1957) tries to play golf two or three times a week and sports a 13 handicap.

While Gregory's father, Walter Kelser Jr., passed away in 1984, his mother (Verna) and brother (Ray) live in nearby Southfield, and he enjoys spending plenty of quality time with them.

Tucson's Home Now

Six years after transferring from Arizona to Michigan State, Gregory "Boobie" Lloyd decided to give Tucson one more shot.

It was 1983, and armed with a pair of degrees from MSU, Lloyd headed back to Arizona without a job.

It was a decision he never regretted!

The year 1984 turned out to be a big one for Gregory.

He landed a job with Federal Express and got married that year, and both are still going strong.

The lightning-quick reserve guard on the Spartans' 1979 NCAA championship squad works at FedEx as a courier/ salesman. In 1991, Lloyd started his own janitorial business as well.

The Lansing Eastern High product earned a bachelor's degree in telecommunications in 1980 and then added a master's degree in fine arts in 1982 from Michigan State.

Gregory and his wife, Veronica, have two children—Whitney (10-3-90) and Omar (11-17-97).

In his spare time, Lloyd likes to help his daughter with her soccer and take his son fishing.

Gregory acquired the nickname "Boobie" when he was a baby, and few people knew his real name until high school when teachers began calling him "Gregory."

"Nobody ever called me Gregory, not even my folks," he said. "When I went to Arizona, it kind of disappeared, but when I came back to Michigan State I was 'Boobie' again.

"Even now when I go home, I'm 'Boobie' to most people."

Hard Work Pays Off for Longaker

Mike Longaker was THE student on Michigan State's basketball team in 1978-79.

Oh, there were other good students, but Longaker carried a 3.9 GPA when he graduated in 1980 with a degree in physiology.

He's now Dr. Mike Longaker, professor of surgery and director of children's surgical research at the Stanford School of Medicine and the Lucile Packard Children's Hospital.

"I consider myself the luckiest guy in the world," said Longaker. "Stanford is a wonderful place to work."

Longaker primarily does research and is on the cutting edge of medical breakthroughs.

"We're taking stem cells and coaching them to become tissues and organs," Longaker said. "It's a form of replacement biology for children without certain organs or with deficient ones."

Longaker had never been in a lab in his life until he worked with Dr. Michael Harrison, who was the first person to operate on an embryo.

"It was a matter of being at the right place at the right time," Longaker said. "It sparked my whole career by that opportunity."

Longaker's medical career has taken him from coast to coast a couple of times. The Warren High product began at the Harvard Medical School, graduating in 1984.

He then spent nine years at the University of California-San Francisco. The first five were in general surgery and the next four postdoctoral in fetal treatment.

Longaker went to New York University in Manhattan from 1993-95, where he practiced reconstructive surgery, and went to UCLA in 1995-96 working in craniofacial.

It was back to New York from 1996-2000, where Longaker was the John Marquis Converse professor at the NYU School of Medicine, directing surgical research.

He assumed his current position at Stanford in 2000.

After all of that, Longaker took evening classes to get a master's degree in business in a program offered jointly by Columbia University and the University of California-Berkeley.

"I do a lot of fundraising with the Packard Foundation, and I wanted to participate more with that," Longaker explained.

Longaker and his wife, Dr. Melinda Longaker, were married in 1988, and they have two sons, Daniel (9-8-99), and Andrew (8-29-02).

Melinda is a dermatologist. They met while both were in residency at the University of California-San Francisco.

As for hobbies, Longaker (born 3-6-58) doesn't have any other than spending as much time as possible with his wife and sons.

Still Lacking 12 Credits

Jay Vincent vows that he will still get his college degree. Right now, though, he's just too busy running V & V Corporation and its five subsidiary companies.

"I tell all the young people I come in contact with that you need a college degree," said Vincent, who is 12 credits shy of his degree at Michigan State.

"I promised myself that one day I'll go back and get it."

In the meantime, Vincent splits his time between the Lansing area and Charlotte, N.C., where he owns Foreclosures Plus. It's a company he started in 1999 that does a lucrative business in foreclosures.

"I've been in the real estate business since 1981, and I've owned as many as 96 houses in Lansing," Vincent said. "I've sold some of them off and moved into the foreclosure business.

"I was looking to find a place where it was warm and I could do real estate. I didn't want Las Vegas or Texas. Charlotte was perfect because it had nice weather and was the second fastest-growing city in the country behind Las Vegas."

Being his own boss allows Vincent the freedom he needs to travel.

"I love going where there's a beach and a little nightlife," Vincent said.

He also enjoys playing blackjack, and don't challenge him to a game of chess.

"I used to play roulette when I was on the road during my NBA days, but a couple of teammates [Michael Adams and Rolando Blackman] got me into blackjack," Vincent said. "It's just a hobby, but I'm pretty good at it.

"I've been playing chess since I was 11 years old. I played all of the time in the NBA, especially on long trips. I didn't lose many times."

Vincent also likes to bowl, but a broken finger sustained during his pro career limits the number of games he can bowl.

Now that he's shaved his head and packs a solid 250 pounds on his 6'8" frame, Vincent has been mistaken for Shaquille O'Neal.

"It's happened a few times," Vincent laughed. "But that guy is really big."

Vincent is the proud father of three children—sons Jayson (20) and Julius (18), and daughter Jayla (one).

Two Setbacks
in Vincent's Life

J ay Vincent winced when I asked the question.
"Does it bother you that if it weren't for Earvin Johnson,
you'd might be known as the greatest basketball player ever to
come out of the Lansing area?"

He'd heard it many times before.

The former Spartan standout from Lansing Eastern looked
me right in the eye and said, "I'm not one bit jealous of Mag. He
went on to be one of the greatest basketball players of all time.

"You know what was hard on me, though? It was that my
father died when I was 12, and I didn't have him when I was
growing up. Earvin had a father who was there all the time."

Jay suffered another major loss in his life in November of
1999 when his biggest fan, brother Jesse, died at the young age
of 45 from complications from asthma.

"That was painful for me because he was always there
supporting me," Vincent said. "I've looked at life totally different
since then. It's toughened me up."

—*Fred Stabley Jr.*

CHAPTER 8

The Coaches

Retirement

Jud Heathcote was born in May of 1927 (he doesn't like the exact birth date revealed all that much), meaning he was 51 years old when the Spartans won the NCAA championship in 1979.

Jud finally retired after the 1995 season, and he nearly stepped down the year before. But the Spartans had a good team returning in '95 with Eric Snow and Shawn Respert leading the way, and Jud also wanted to make sure the world knew he wasn't being forced out by anyone following the '94 season. So he stayed on for another year past his original retirement plan.

Jud and wife Beverly decided they did not want to keep up two households, so they decided to move to Spokane, Washington, to be near their daughters. They built their dream home, and both are happy with the setup.

Since the basketball world knew when Jud was stepping aside, each Big Ten school honored him when the Spartans paid a visit. Jud told his staff and players to focus on the game at hand and let him deal with the distractions of his retirement ceremonies.

Jud was touched by athletic director Joe Roberson and the tribute he was paid when the Spartans played at Michigan. He received gifts from them all.

I worked the telecast of the game the Spartans played at Indiana, where Jud's friend, Bob Knight, took to the microphone prior to the opening tip. Knight glared at Jud as he walked to center court, where he presented him with a chair with an engraving— "To Jud Heathcote, with great respect, from Indiana University."

Jud received a huge ovation when he took the mike and kept it short and sweet. "Thanks, Bob—you're a great friend and a great coach." Words to that effect. Then Indiana went out and beat the Spartans silly that night.

Jud was surprised at the reception he received from the various fans, but in hindsight he remembered that he had spoken at all of the booster luncheons on the road at one time or another and obviously they laughed as MSU fans had done for years at his one-liners.

"Knight or Keady would receive the same reception I did if everyone knew a year in advance when they were stepping down, Jud says. "The people in the Midwest are good basketball fans and very knowledgeable. They appreciated the competition we gave their teams over the years and they recognized the other side of me."

Today, Jud dotes on his three grandchildren. He has a satellite dish at home and watches the Spartans play when he doesn't attend their games in person. He always attends the Final Fours with Bev. He visits with Tom Izzo on the telephone on numerous occasions. He also attends the home games of Gonzaga University, located in Spokane.

Jud was offered speaking engagements, clinics and camp appearances immediately after his retirement and turned most of them down. He was tired of the travel and was ready for retirement.

He misses playing competitive handball, which he had to give up in 2001 because of health reasons. Jud has had a hip replacement among other fixes and, of course, he survived a heart attack while he was coaching.

"I've outlived my body," he kids to those who ask how he is feeling.

Jud always loves to compete and still enjoys golf when he feels up to it. The 19th hole after any round offers him an enjoyable social outlet where he loves to be around friends.

When he left Michigan State, Jud was offered some television work from the Big Sky Conference. But Jud remembered his days at Montana and all of those long flights in bad weather through small airports. He passed on all of the television offers.

He was given a lifetime membership to his East Lansing country club, Walnut Hills, and he still enjoys visiting with friends there in the summer. The club felt it owed Jud the favor after all of the impromptu speeches he agreed to make at the various club events, free of charge, over the years.

Big Money!

Jud Heathcote never coached to make money. If he had, who knows how much loot he could have pocketed. As a speaker, he could have commanded sums that others could only dream of. His ability to ad lib, to improvise, to charm, to cajole, and to make people laugh was as famous as his head-thumping routine on the sideline during games.

But money was never a big issue with Jud. He lived in the same upper middle-class home in East Lansing for his entire career. He had a country club membership and a car, but very few other perks.

When he arrived at Michigan State, his four-year contract covered all of one piece of paper. He accepted a $25,000 annual salary, plus control of the summer camps for additional income and any money he could make from a television show.

"My salary was a bigger issue to my wife Bev than it was to me," Jud says today. "I often felt I was getting paid more than I should. I felt like I was a professor, because I taught classes as well as coached and my salary, I felt, should remain in line with comparable professors' earnings."

Jud Heathcote and Bobby Knight share a moment away from the floor. Incidentally, Michigan State defeated the Hoosiers three times in 1978-79—the only time a Knight-coached Indiana team lost three games to the same team in one season. *Photo courtesy of MSU Sports Information*

By the time Jud's second season rolled around, 1978-79, his salary had "skyrocketed" all the way to $33,000 per year. And was there any bonus for winning the NCAA title? You betcha! Another six grand. Jud soared to $39,000 after the Spartans beat Indiana State in Salt Lake City!

Forever a Coach?

It's not true that Bill Berry has been coaching basketball since Moby Dick was a minnow ... it just seems that way. The former Michigan State assistant on the 1979 NCAA championship team completed his 38th season this past spring.

"It doesn't seem that long, but time flies," said Berry. "I plan to coach until I don't enjoy it any longer."

A 1964 graduate of Michigan State, Berry spent four years as a high school coach following college. He came back to MSU and earned a master's degree in physical education in 1969 while helping coach the Spartans.

Berry then became head coach at Cosumnes River JC for two years and served as an assistant at the University of California for the next five years before returning to his alma mater for two seasons—two Big Ten titles and one NCAA crown.

"That was certainly one of the most exciting times in my life," Berry said. "Coaching and working with the players on that team was special."

Berry left East Lansing following the championship season and spent the next 10 years as the head coach at San Jose State. His teams were 142-144, compiling the second highest win total in school history. He led his teams to berths in the NCAA and NIT tournaments.

He went to the pro ranks in 1989 and has been there ever since—two years as an assistant with Sacramento, eight years with Houston and the past four with Chicago.

Bill and his wife, Reese, were married on Dec. 12, 1963, and currently call Chicago home. Their daughter, Pam, is married and lives in Houston with a son, Tyler.

Berry enjoys hunting, fishing and playing golf in his spare time.

"I love playing golf," he said. "Rudy Tomjanovich [Houston's former head coach] got me into it."

Because of his coaching demands, Berry has not made it back to Michigan State as much as he would like.

"I got back for the reunion in 1989, but that's been it," he said.

How did the 6'2" forward from Winnemucca, Nev., ever become a Spartan in the first place?

"We had a player from my school named David Cox who got a scholarship to Michigan State the year before me," Berry said. "We won back-to-back state titles. He paved the way for me to go there, too."

World's Best?

That's what assistant coach Bill Berry claimed after Michigan State's 75-64 win over Indiana State in the 1979 NCAA finals.

"We beat Brazil and the Russians and now we win the NCAA championship," Berry said. "We could make a legitimate claim to be the best amateur basketball team in the world."

The Spartans had defeated Brazil, 96-94, in the finals of the Governor's Cup in Sao Paulo, Brazil in September before clobbering the Russian Nationals at home, 76-60, in an impressive exhibition win early in November.

MSU fans would certainly agree with Berry's statement.

Best Ever?

There have been many great NCAA basketball champions throughout the years, but Dave Harshman would pit the 1979 Spartans against any of them.

"I'd put our team against them all," said Harshman, a first-year assistant on that team. "We had one of the greatest players and ball handlers of all time in Earvin Johnson, a tremendous college player in Gregory Kelser and another talented 6'8" guy in Jay Vincent, who had an excellent NBA career.

"Plus, we had support players who knew their role and fulfilled them. It was a close-knit group, one with a sense of family. They've all gone on to be successful in life."

Harshman cherishes those memories more with each passing year.

"I can remember Jud Heathcote saying that the older we became, the more special that 1979 season would become," Harshman said. "I still talk to some of the guys."

Harshman, whose father, Marv Harshman, was a legendary coach at Washington State and Washington, has remained active in basketball.

In February of 2002, Dave became the head coach at Pacific Lutheran (Tacoma, Wash.), a Division III school that his father coached to prominence before moving on to the two Washington schools.

It's a program with no scholarships. How will he recruit? "I guess I'll have to use my winning personality," he laughed.

Prior to taking the Pacific Lutheran post, Dave spent 12 years as a color commentator doing Pac-10 and Western Athletic Conference games for Fox Sports Northwest.

In addition, Dave ran a program called Hoops With Heart that helped develop young basketball players down to 12 years old. He also had summer camps for big men and perimeter players and took summer teams to the Adidas Big Time tourney in Las Vegas.

Seven girls from Harshman's program earned Division I scholarships in 2001-02.

After leaving Michigan State in 1982, Harshman had two stints as an assistant coach with the Seattle Supersonics and was the head coach for the Wisconsin Flyers of the CBA. He was an assistant at Lamar University for the 1986-87 season and was an assistant with Washington State from 1987-89.

Dave and his wife, MaryAnn, live in Tacoma. They have seven children.

First Meeting

Dave Harshman had just sunk two free throws to ice a big upset win for Pullman High over Spokane's University High, and he was celebrating in the locker room with his teammates.

The door opened and in walked Jud Heathcote, the coach of West Valley High.

"I had never met him before, but I knew who it was the second he walked in," Harshman recalled.

Heathcote walked straight over to him, shook his hand and said, "Jud Heathcote … lucky shot."

He then turned around and walked out.

"Things went downhill in our relationship from then on," joked Harshman.

Heathcote ended up coaching under Dave's father, Marv Harshman, for seven years at Washington State. Dave played for him on a freshman team that lost only one game.

In fact, Heathcote's five freshmen teams at WSU went an incredible 99-9.

"Jud was like another father to me," said Harshman who ended up on Heathcote's staff at Michigan State. "I learned so much about basketball and how to compete from him."

There's something called "Jud's Rules," as his friends are quick to point out.

"Like in golf, for example, you can't be anywhere behind him or you're in his line of sight," Dave said. "Even if you're 100 yards away! When you're hitting, he could be anywhere. It didn't matter then."

"Jud's Rules" also carried over to the basketball floor in pickup games at WSU when Marv Harshman and baseball coach Bobo Brayton would have regular battles with Heathcote and another guy. The offensive player, according to the rules, had the option of calling a foul.

One time, with the game on the line, Brayton drove to the hoop and Heathcote did everything but a chin up on his arm. Brayton bulled his way for the winning basketball.

Heathcote screamed that he had committed a foul. Brayton refused to call it, and that was the end of the two-on-two matches.

The younger Harshman also remembers an All-Star game at the end of a summer camp when Marv Harshman and Jud were coaching against each other. One of the referees was his good buddy, Bobo.

"Well, it got quite heated, and you know how intense Jud can be. Bobo called one or two technical fouls on Jud and threatened to throw him out of the gym," Dave said. "That was vintage Jud, ever the competitor."

Heathcote: Hall of Famer?

Former Michigan State assistant coach Dave Harshman is outspoken in his praise of Spartans basketball coach Jud Heathcote.

"Jud should be in the the Hall of Fame, there's no question about it," said Harshman, an assistant to Heathcote on the 1979 NCAA championship squad. "Jud never got the credit he deserved. He was one of the great bench coaches in the game.

"He had an amazing ability to analyze players' strengths and weaknesses, and he was an outstanding shooting instructor."

Heathcote's record backs up Harshman's contention.

Not only did he prove himself at Michigan State, but his five teams at Montana went 80-53 and his 1974-75 club won the Grizzlies' first Big Sky Conference title. That team posted a 21-8 mark and lost in the regional finals to eventual NCAA champion UCLA by three points.

Heathcote's second team at MSU went 25-5, setting a school record for wins, and then lost in the regional finals to eventual

NCAA champ, Kentucky. His third team broke the school mark for wins again with 26 and copped the NCAA title.

In 19 years with the Spartans, Jud's teams posted a record of 340-220 (.607) and captured three Big Ten titles. His career mark was 420-273 (.606) in 24 seasons at two schools not known for their basketball prowess prior to Heathcote's reign.

Dave just might have a point.

Fred Paulsen

F red Paulsen is still amazed when he thinks about it.
"When the best two players on your team are also your hardest workers ... that just blows me away," said Paulsen, a restricted earnings coach for Michigan State's 1979 NCAA basketball championship team. "The chemistry on that team was so good because of those two. They took care of a lot of little problems that all teams have.

"That championship run was a player's thing. I give Jud a lot of credit because he prepared them for each game and then let them play."

The two with the incredible work ethic were Earvin Johnson and Gregory Kelser.

Paulsen took off on his own the following year and spent one season at Montana Tech as the head coach before going to Alpena (Mich.) Junior College and then Anoka-Ramsey (Coon Rapids, Minn.) J. C.

The Dowagiac (Mich.) High product then settled in at Huron University (Huron, S.D.) from 1984-90. He went to Penn State-Behrend from 1990-93 before returning to Huron from 1993-97. His Huron teams were 180-119 and reached the NAIA tourney four times.

Paulsen, who got a bachelor's degree from Northern Montana College and his master's from the United States Sports Academy, moved to Custer (S.D.) in 1997 as the dean of students and associate basketball coach. The two Custer teams he helped coach went 46-6, winning the Class A state title in 1998 and finishing third in '99.

Fred still coaches AAU ball and helps out with the Custer team.

He spent 17 years as a head coach and posted a record of 260-197, accumulating a postseason mark of 23-9.

Paulsen and his wife, Marilyn (married in 1976), have two children, Paige and Spencer. A third son, Derek, was tragically killed in an automobile accident in the summer of 1999, which helped curtail his coaching career.

In his spare time, Fred likes to fish, play golf and coach.

A Spartan Tragedy

Many members of the Spartan basketball family have been featured in *Sports Illustrated* since the 1979 NCAA championship.

Most of them have been positive, welcomed stories. Who doesn't want to be written up in *SI*?

Fred Paulsen, the restricted earning coach from that team, is one who would have preferred never seeing his name in print. Not this way.

When doing research for this book, I asked him how many children he had. "Two walking and one flying," he responded.

When I asked what he meant by that, he said that his oldest son, Derek, was killed in an automobile accident. He said that there was a story in the February 21, 2000 issue of *Sports Illustrated* that explained everything.

The story took up five pages and had a headline that read, "Custer's Fallen Warrior."

Fred's son was a 6'4", 190-pound guard prospect from Custer, S.D., who was being recruited by Michigan State, Marquette, North Carolina State, Northwestern and Princeton, among others. Quite amazing when you consider that Custer High School had never produced a Division I athlete.

In the summer of 1999, Derek and his longtime girlfriend, Eva Wahlstrom, were killed when they were hit head on by a car going an estimated 100 miles per hour.

"Fourteen hundred people attended the memorial services," the story in *SI* said. "Derek and Eva, the best and the brightest, were laid to rest side by side in a small cemetery in Hermosa, her hometown, on a slope overlooking the Black Hills. She'd taken Derek there the day before the accident to show him the view from the plot where she wanted to be buried. Now it was their view, forever."

The Paulsens have coped the best they can.

"For us, the accident is like yesterday," Fred said in the *SI* story. "I think of him every day. I'm bitter at happy occasions. I ask why. Why us?

"Life is precious. That's the only thing I can tell people about this. How quickly it can be snuffed out boggles the mind."

The Spartan family mourns with the Paulsens.

—*Fred Stabley Jr.*

Payne Leaves His Mark

When doing research for this book, one name kept coming up as a key ingredient in the building of Michigan State's 1979 NCAA basketball championship team.

It was a person who wasn't there to cut the nets in Salt Lake City or put on a championship ring.

But Vern Payne may have been the most important person not present when the Spartans walked off with the trophy.

Payne was an assistant coach with Jud Heathcote for one season before moving on to become the head coach at Wayne State and, subsequently, Western Michigan.

"I was very happy and proud of whatever role I played in the success of that team," said Payne, now an assistant vice president of student affairs at Western Michigan.

All the personable Payne did was play a prominent role in signing Ron Charles, Gregory Kelser and Earvin Johnson. And then discourage the disenchanted Charles and Kelser from transferring.

"When I first came to Michigan State, I had the opportunity to work for Gus Ganakas," Payne said. "Gus had such a love for Michigan State, and I slowly began to understand his feelings.

"He felt Michigan State was bigger than himself and the players. He preached it and lived it. He always wanted what was best for Michigan State."

When Ganakas was removed from his job after the 1975-76 season, many of the players were upset by the decision.

"My message to them then was that they had committed to Michigan State and that they had to honor that," Payne said.

After one year with the oftentimes volatile Heathcote, Charles and Kelser were considering going elsewhere.

"It was readily apparent that they were going to struggle with Jud as a person," Payne said. "But I felt they would become the best basketball players possible under Jud. The one thing I understood after spending one year as his assistant was that the man could flat-out coach.

"I regret that I wasn't around to get a ring, but I don't regret that I encouraged them to stay. I was confident that the program was going to turn around."

Before heading off to Wayne State, Payne had one more job—get Earvin Johnson to become a Spartan.

"I met with Earvin in the library at Lansing Everett," Payne said. "It was at 7:30 in the morning and we talked for about an hour.

"I told him that he was 'Magic' right here, and it was important to the people in Lansing and East Lansing that he stayed home. He could go someplace else and not be 'Magic.' He had built programs wherever he'd gone and that it would be no different at Michigan State."

Two days later, Earvin told the world he'd be wearing the green and white.

Payne spent five years as the head coach at Wayne State and seven more at Western Michigan. He and his wife, Dorphine, live in Kalamazoo and are plenty busy with their five grandkids—four of whom live nearby.

CHAPTER 9

The Support Staff

Kearney Enjoys Retired Life in Tucson

Joe Kearney was Michigan State's athletics director for just four years, and he drew much criticism from the Spartan faithful when he left in 1980 for the AD post at Arizona State.

Some zealots even went so far as to call him a "carpet-bagger."

However, a closer look at Kearney's stay in East Lansing shows it was extremely productive.

When Kearney took over on April 1, 1976, Michigan State was in the throes of probationary status. In 1978-79, the Spartans won Big Ten championships in football, basketball and baseball and then captured their first-ever NCAA basketball championship.

His Spartan legacy grows greater when you remember the head coaches he brought to East Lansing–Darryl Rogers in football, Jud Heathcote in basketball and Ron Mason in hockey.

Kearney spent only a few months at Arizona State before the Western Athletic Conference made an offer "he couldn't refuse." He served as the commissioner of the WAC from 1980-94 when he retired.

Although Joe had retired in 1994, he completed a 16-year volunteer stint on the United States Olympic Committee with the 2000 Olympic Games in Sydney. He was chairman of the International Games Preparation Committee.

Kearney had the opportunity to renew old acquaintances with Earvin Johnson at the 1992 Olympics in Barcelona when Magic was playing for the USA basketball team.

"Earvin was awfully busy, but we did get a chance to reminisce about the 1979 NCAA championship," said Kearney, who was born on April 28, 1927 in Pittsburgh, Pa. "We had a nice time together."

While Kearney retired in Tucson, Ariz., where he lives on the Tucson National Golf Course, he's far from idle.

"I do some consulting as well as volunteer work with the National Football College Hall of Fame," said Kearney.

Joe and his wife, Dorothea, also keep busy with their five children and 11 grandkids who live in Scottsdale, Portland, Denver, Wyoming and Switzerland. "We need a travel agent to keep in touch with all of them," Kearney laughed.

In his spare time, Kearney said, "I also putz around with golf, but I'm not very good at it."

Great Hires!

If the effectiveness of an administrator is measured by who he/she hires, then give Joe Kearney an A+.

As Michigan State's athletics director in the late 1970s, Kearney brought in Ron Mason (hockey), Darryl Rogers (football) and Jud Heathcote (basketball) as head coaches.

Mason became the winningest college hockey coach in history, Rogers won a Big Ten title before moving on to Arizona

State and the Detroit Lions, and Heathcote helped resurrect Spartan basketball.

Kearney had an interesting philosophy in hiring a head coach.

"I always wanted to have three people lined up," said Kearney "I wanted to be as thrilled with the first person as I was the third."

Looking at who Kearney hired, he must have been ecstatic.

His three head football hires as an AD were Jim Owens, Don James and Rogers, while his three head basketball coaches hires were a trio of legends in Tex Winter, Marv Harshman and Heathcote.

"I knew Jud for a long time and was convinced at what he could do for a basketball program," said Kearney.

"We coached against each other [Kearney was the freshman coach at Washington and Heathcote at Washington State], and I kept following his career."

Kearney brought Jud in from the University of Montana, where he'd posted a record of 80-53 in five years.

Jud coached the Spartans for 19 years and had a record of 340-220 (.607). His teams won one NCAA crown and three Big Ten titles.

NCAA Championship No. 1

My father, the late Fred Stabley Sr., surprised a lot of people in the early 1980s when he was asked about his most memorable moment in athletics after 32 years as the sports information director at Michigan State.

Some thought it could have been any of three Rose Bowls his beloved Spartans played in or the 10-10 football tie with Notre Dame in 1966. Others were sure it came when he worked the 1980 Olympics and watched the United States win the gold medal in hockey after the improbable win over the Soviet Union.

Nope! It was Michigan State's 1979 NCAA championship in basketball.

The late Fred Stabley Sr., Michigan State's sports information director for 32 years, called the Spartans' NCAA Championship in 1979 his No. 1 moment in sports. Behind'"Butler" was his assistant of 25 years, Nick Vista (left), and another former Spartan assistant SID, the late Ted Emery. *Photo courtesy of MSU Sports Information*

"Nothing compared to the thrill and the drama of winning the NCAA title," he said. "The anticipation ... the excitement ... the 'Magic' of the moment was like nothing else.

"The tournament run was wonderful, and then you had two of the greatest basketball players ever in the finals and a captivated national TV audience watching college athletics at its best. The media demand was incredible. I loved every minute of it."

My dad had been there in late 1957 when the Spartans and Jumpin' Johnny Green lost in a controversial triple-overtime game to North Carolina in the NCAA semis.

MSU made no doubt about it this time around. Dad was pleased.

—*Fred Stabley Jr.*

A Little Help from a Friend

Nick Vista was not supposed to be in Salt Lake City for the 1979 NCAA championship tilt between his beloved Michigan State Spartans and Indiana State.

The assistant sports information director at MSU was slated to be the press host at the NCAA hockey tourney in Detroit at the same time. However, the late Tom Greenhoe of Minnesota offered to take over Vista's chores, allowing Nick to head West.

"It worked out great for both of us," said Vista, now retired and living in suburban Atlanta with his wife, Connie. "We won the NCAA basketball title, and Tom's team defeated North Dakota for the NCAA hockey crown."

The Spartan championship was a career highlight for the affable Vista.

"The final accomplishment in Salt Lake City was the top experience in my 33 years in sports information at Michigan State," Vista said. "I've always said that going to a Final Four is a great thrill, and going there with your team is even greater, and being there when your team wins it all is the greatest!"

Vista became MSU's head SID in July of 1980 and remained in that position until June of 1988 when he joined his wife in Georgia, where she had accepted a position as associate vice president for university relations at Emory University.

While Nick retired, he didn't become inactive.

He started volunteer work in 1989 with the Atlanta Sports Council, an arm of the Atlanta Chamber of Commerce, and he's been involved in sports there ever since. In 1994, Nick came out of retirement to join the communications staff of the Atlanta Committee for the 1996 Olympic Games.

Vista has served as a press conference moderator for a number of NCAA regional basketball events and worked the 2002 NCAA Finals in Atlanta in the same capacity.

Nick and Connie try to get back to Michigan State as often as possible but also enjoy spending time with their two grandsons, who live in the Atlanta area, and going to their cabin in the mountains of north Georgia.

But the Spartans are never far from the Battle Creek native's mind.

"I remain a great and loyal Spartan follower," said Vista who recently turned 78. "And I bleed a lot of green."

Belloli:
The Man Behind the Cage

E d Belloli spent eight years in a "cage" and loved every minute of it.

After 30 years as a firefighter in St. Louis, Missouri, Ed and his wife, Marie, decided to move to East Lansing to spend time with his son, Tom, and his grandchildren.

That's where Ed stumbled on the "job of a lifetime" as Michigan State's equipment manager for basketball. His "office" was the caged equipment room outside the men's locker room on the ground level of Jenison Field House.

"I loved it," Belloli said. "It gave me something to do in retirement, and everyone treated me great. They made me feel a part of the team. I had a great relationship with everyone.

"In fact, I'd have stayed on much longer except that Marie wanted to start traveling like I'd promised her we would."

Belloli left Michigan State in 1980, one year after the Spartans captured the NCAA title, and spent the next 20 years traveling until Marie passed away in October of 2000.

"We took the kids and grandkids with us on one cruise," Belloli said. "We enjoyed ourselves more since moving to East Lansing than we did in St. Louis."

A big reason for that was his relationship with Michigan State.

"Michigan State treated me better when I retired than the fire department did," he said. "The people there never forgot me and always included me in everything."

The white-haired Belloli always had an easy-going personality that allowed him to get along well with people.

"I really liked working with the players," Belloli said. "I had high respect for all of them."

Two who stood out, however, were Mike and Donnie Brkovich.

"They were great kids," Belloli said. "They stopped by the cage every day and talked, and when they went on trips they'd often bring me back a T-shirt or something. That wasn't necessary, but I sure appreciated it."

Belloli didn't normally travel, although the Spartans did take him to Salt Lake City for the NCAA finals.

"You had to go through it to understand what it meant," Belloli said. "I'd spent so much time with those guys and then to watch them win the title. It was great."

Born in St. Louis on Jan. 6, 1916, Belloli loves hunting, fishing and playing golf, although his golf game "stinks." His real love from a lad on was soccer, and he coached youth soccer into his 80s.

Ed lives in Haslett with his son, Tom, and daughter-in-law, Sally, and escapes the snowy winters by spending time at Pompano Beach in Florida.

"We kind of have a shrine to Michigan State on the lower level of our house," Belloli said. "All of the trophies and plaques I got at Michigan State are there along with Tom and Sally's. They were soccer and field hockey players at MSU."

Belloli has enjoyed watching his three grandkids play soccer and now hopes to be able to see his great-grandchild play one day.

Knight Erupts, Belloli Laughs

Ed Belloli didn't care much for Indiana's tempestuous Bob Knight. And when the Hoosier mentor chewed him out, it just supported his feelings.

Michigan State was remodeling the locker room area in Jenison Field House, and Jud Heathcote told the Spartan basketball equipment manager to put visiting Indiana in the women's locker room.

"I had nothing to do with it, but Knight came and chewed me out anyway," Belloli recalled. "I just told him that he needed to take it up with Jud.

"I never cared much for him to begin with; I just didn't like the way he treated his players, but that clinched it. Actually, I thought it was quite funny. When he stormed away, I had a good laugh over the whole thing."

Analysis From Gus

Who knows how Michigan State's teams would have fared had Gus Ganakas remained the Spartans' head coach following the 1975 season. He was busy recruiting Earvin Johnson out of Lansing Everett, and it was considered a lock that the two would get together at Michigan State. When Gus was removed as head coach, Earvin considered other schools, and it got to nail-biting time in the spring of Earvin's senior year in high school before he finally eliminated Michigan and chose to become a Spartan instead.

Gus ended up serving as the analyst for WJIM-TV in Lansing, which televised ten games in each of Earvin's two seasons.

"I was impressed with the soundness of the 1979 team," Gus recalls. "Kelser was a star and the others were role players and, of course, those roles weren't as difficult because of Earvin's presence.

"Their matchup zone was great with Kelser, Vincent, and Charles on the base line with Earvin getting down there now and then."

Gus cites the Ohio State game in Jenison when Earvin made his famous second-half return from an ankle injury as his most memorable game of that season.

What's It All Mean?

So what have the two national championships in basketball done for Michigan State's overall national image?

Thoughts from Gus Ganakas, head coach from 1969-76 and the predecessor to Jud Heathcote:

"It was big then [1979] and bigger now [2000]," Ganakas says.

"It was big in the late '50s when Johnny Green led the Spartans deep into the tournament. Winning the national championship any more continues to grow in prestige for any school that wins it.

"These two teams put Michigan State on the basketball map. Then having Magic do what he's done since then has elevated us to prominence nationally. Tom [Izzo] has built on what Earvin did. Winning in 2000 was the zenith."

A Coach Remembers

Friends still chuckle over Gus's dismissal. He was called to President Clifton Wharton's home on a Sunday afternoon following the season thinking he might be in line for a raise. Instead, he was being replaced as head basketball coach. Gus had tenure, so he was given a job in the athletic department.

Jud was always complimentary of Gus through the years for showing no rancor toward his successor and offering only support. Gus talked his prized holdover player, Gregory Kelser, into staying in school and not transferring. A coach named Dick Vitale was at the University of Detroit at the time and was looking to get Kelser to return to his hometown and play for the Titans. Even though Heathcote had not been appointed yet, Gus convinced Kelser that he should remain a Spartan.

When Joe Kearney came to Michigan State as athletic director, he created a program called the Spartan Scouts and placed Gus in charge. Kearney and Ganakas would travel around

Michigan and neighboring states informing boosters of what they could and could not do. They worked with alumni on departmental relations and visited various high schools. They also sought summer jobs for athletes, and it was an activity that kept Gus busy.

Gus joined Tim Staudt to do the telecasts of MSU basketball during the 1978 and 1979 seasons. WJIM-TV in Lansing was the local originator of the ten-game season package, and Gus was hired to do the color. He and Jud were cordial even though Gus did not spend a great deal of time visiting with Jud. Their offices were close, but Gus learned more about team news from Jud's assistant coaches than from the head man himself.

After Kearney left for Arizona State with football coach Darryl Rogers in December, 1979, Gus found new duties under incoming athletic director Doug Weaver.

The Spartan Scout program folded under Weaver, and Gus worked to sell advertising in the various publications of the department. He also handled administrative duties for the winter/ spring teams that were considered non-revenue sports.

Gus has continued to stay close to the basketball program through the years. He became Tom Izzo's director of operations before retiring from the university in July, 2001. He still serves as the analyst on the radio broadcasts and has done so for a number of years.

Spartan Trainer Savors NCAA Title

Clint Thompson served as a trainer on three national championship teams in his 37 years in the business.

But nothing compared to Michigan State's NCAA basketball championship in 1979.

"From a personal standpoint, that was the best," Thompson said. "There's fewer athletes and you get to know them better.

"It was amazing to me how fast Jud turned things around. He took over a program that needed to win and he got it done."

Thompson was a student trainer at the University of Texas early in the 1960s when the Longhorns won a national football championship, and he was an assistant trainer to the legendary Gayle Robinson at Michigan State when the Spartan gridders were national champs in 1966.

Thompson retired in the summer of 2001 and moved with his wife, Kathy, to Seattle, Wash., when she got a job as a trainer for the Washington Huskies.

A graduate of Texas, Thompson was an assistant at MSU from 1964-70 before going to Colorado State for three years. He then returned to MSU in 1973 and served as the head trainer until 1985.

After a brief journey into the private sector, Thompson finished his training career at Northeast Missouri State (aka Truman State) from 1985-2001.

Although he's retired, Thompson is more active now than ever in the National Athletic Trainers Association (NATA). He serves on four committees.

"I'm enjoying myself and I don't really see anything changing in the future," Thompson said.

In addition to being a "housekeeper" while his wife continues to work, Thompson is into computers, reading, music, photography and a lot of outdoor things like biking.

Sometimes, though, he reflects back on his days with Spartan basketball.

"Jud was such a unique person and that made for a great learning experience," Thompson said. "And I don't mean that in a negative way. It was fun to watch this team win and win big."

Gentleman Jim

Jim Adams was used to dealing with easy-going coaches during his years broadcasting Michigan State basketball from the late 1940s to the day Jud Heathcote arrived on campus back in the spring of 1976.

Adams was the voice of the school's radio station, and he loved basketball. He forged close relationships with coaches like Forddy Anderson, John Benington and Gus Ganakas along the way. All enjoyed basketball chat sessions in the coaches' offices with Adams at any time of the year.

Adams was invited to breakfast at the Kellogg Center the morning Heathcote was introduced at a press conference along with new football coach Darryl Rogers. After five minutes of conversation, Adams thought to himself, "Who in the world have we hired?"

Jud was a personality change from his predecessors. He was funny, but he was moody too, and Adams was always in an easygoing frame of mind. They became friends, but the long chat sessions in Heathcote's office were few and far between.

Adams called games on radio through the '82-'83 season, when a network was formed, and that ended his play-by-play duties. He eventually retired from the university in August of 1993.

Recalling the 1979 team, Adams said he was surprised so many of the players went on to professions still involving the world of sports. And he was amazed at Earvin Johnson's demeanor with Heathcote.

"We came out of a restaurant one time during a trip in North Carolina," Adams recalled. "Earvin was walking down the street with his arms around Jud's shoulders. I was walking behind. I thought that no other player could get away with such a casual demeanor with a coach like Jud.

"His practices were tough. I thought it was too bad more people didn't see Jud's softer side through the years because some fans were glad to see him leave despite his success."

Adams believes the '79 team had a huge impact on college basketball and Michigan State University.

"Earvin was on television a great deal, and most times we won," Adams said. "Other players saw how he played and wanted to imitate him. And when Kelser, Vincent and Earvin all went to the NBA, they continued to spread Michigan State's basketball image."

Adams was always amazed at the clamor around Johnson every time the Spartans made a road trip.

"When we played at North Carolina, an enormous amount of press people showed up just to see Earvin at practice the night before the game," Adams said. "They just wanted to see him shoot a free throw in the gym or make a pass or any other kind of shot. What amazed me is that for all the attention Earvin got, Kelser and Vincent never seemed to show any resentment. Those North Carolina media people thought Earvin was the world's greatest player—some just wanted to touch his jersey."

Adams broadcast MSU's first NCAA tournament game in 1957.

"That was an impressive-looking team. Johnny Green was a great jumper, and Larry Hedden and Jack Quiggle were superb players also. The '79 team had some skinny guys like Kelser and Ron Charles, some scrawny guys like Brkovich and Donnelly, and a beefy guy like Jay. We were not an awesome-looking team in '79, but boy could they play."

Adams observed Jud closely toward the end of his career, which was the 1995-96 season.

"Jud was worried about retirement," Adams said. "He called me in and asked about my retirement and how I liked it. He didn't have a clue as to what he was going to do with his time. And I think Bev [Jud's wife] was more worried than he was."

More than a "Manager"

Darwin Payton always considered himself more than a "manager" for the Michigan State basketball team.

He was also a confidante of the players and a person who had the ear of head coach Jud Heathcote.

"Not many people know this, but I met with Jud before every game to give him a pulse on the team," Payton said. "We'd meet in his room on the road or in his office at home.

"If something was going on that was detrimental to the team, I told him. Of course, there were some things I just couldn't tell

Darwin Payton, the diminutive manager, was a key member of the Spartan family. He had the ear of Jud Heathcote and the confidence of the MSU players. *Photo courtesy of MSU Sports Information*

him at all. Sometimes I'd just tell him that he needed to lighten up on this player or that one."

Payton was as much a counselor as he was a manager.

"They all came to my room and talked," he said. "I helped keep them in line. They'd discuss problems [they had] with Jud or their girlfriend. I don't think I was the typical manager."

Payton has many fond memories of the championship run, but none stick out more than two with Jud.

"One was when the NCAA title was ours against Indiana State, Jud came right to my seat next to the scorer's table and shook my hand and congratulated me before he did anybody else," Payton said. "The other was when he presented me with a special plaque at our team banquet that had never been given to anyone before."

The 5'9" Payton prepped at basketball-rich River Rouge High School, where he earned two letters.

The legendary Rouge basketball coach, Lofton Greene, asked Darwin where he was going to college. Payton told him Michigan State, and Greene said he was a good friend of Spartan hoops mentor Gus Ganakas.

"He called Gus for me and that's how I became a manager," Payton said. "Those were some of the greatest times of my life. You know, if I could go back in time it would be to those days at Michigan State. Earvin and I reminisce a lot about those days.

"My wife [Charlisa] has heard all the stories many times over, but I still love to talk about them."

The "Little Giant" from River Rouge

Earvin Johnson had tried for years to lure Darwin Payton away from the comforts of the Midwest to the hustle and bustle of Los Angeles.

It finally happened in 1984, but not until leukemia had taken the life of his wife of one year, Peggy, who had battled the disease for 14 years before the disease finally won.

Payton was Earvin's personal assistant and ran Magic Johnson Enterprises from 1984-91.

"I pretty much watched Earvin's back," Payton recalled, adding with a chuckle: "People thought I was his bodyguard because I was always there. They thought I was pretty tough, too, because I was only 5'9" and didn't weigh much."

After Magic's HIV announcement in 1991, Earvin became more business-oriented, and his holdings started to grow.

Payton then became executive VP of Magic Johnson Productions and remained in that capacity until April of 1999.

"We were entertainment-driven and we had star-studded events," Payton said. "I'd get all kind of stars calling and asking for tickets. I'd play games with them and tell them that there were few tickets left when there was actually a boxful in front of me.

"I told them I'd see what I could do and would get back to them. I'd call back in 15 minutes and tell them that I'd scraped up four for them. Boy, they loved me. I had a lot of fun doing that."

Darwin formed his own production company, Payton and Payton, in 1999 before becoming the CEO of JCH Development in 2001. It's a company building an upscale community in Palm Springs.

A 1979 graduate of Michigan State in finance, Payton was a graduate assistant for the Spartans in basketball in 1980 and '81. He helped Fred Paulsen coach the junior varsity. Another one of Paulsen's assistants was Kelvin Sampson, who recently vaulted the University of Oklahoma to national prominence.

"We were 33-7 in those two years and we mainly had walk-ons," Payton recalled proudly.

Payton, born April 22, 1957, married again in 1991. He and his wife, Charlisa, live in Altadena, Calif., and have two sons, Darwin Jr. (5-7-92) and Matthew (8-15-94).

In his free time, Darwin enjoys bowling, playing golf, roller skating and taking his family camping.

The "Quiet" Manager

Jud Heathcote always referred to them as "management." They were the managers, the ones who did all of the dirty work that the coaches didn't want to do.

Today, there may be as many as 10 or 12 per team, nearly one per player.

However, in 1978-79, there were just two—the outgoing, bubbly Darwin Payton and the much more quiet and reserved Randy Bishop.

Payton eventually followed his close buddy Earvin Johnson and headed for the bright lights of Los Angeles.

Bishop settled for a more serene setting, returning to his Grand Rapids-area roots.

"Dar was tight with the big guys like Earvin, and he had Jud's confidence," Bishop recalled. "I was a little too quiet and under-confident for Jud, but he stuck with me for that year and the next.

"I have told him that I appreciated the opportunity he gave me to work with that team ... his special team at a special time."

Bishop got married (Jeanine) in the summer following the NCAA championship, and then worked one more season for the Spartans before graduating with a social science/prelaw degree.

After working for a year at a shoe store in his native town of Wyoming, Bishop earned a master's degree in sport administration from Ohio State in 1982. He did an internship working for the Columbus Clippers, a Triple-A team of the New York Yankees, but decided against a career in baseball.

"We already had one child and another was on the way," Bishop said. "We decided not to try for an 'unsure' baseball job someplace in the country."

So they returned to Grand Rapids, and Randy spent four years as an assistant at the same retail shoe store he worked at after college.

"I became restless and started doing some research on careers," Bishop said.

He settled on a career in the insurance business, and has been active since 1987.

Bishop, a 1976 graduate of Wyoming Lee High, and his wife have three children—sons Aharon and Adam, and a daughter, Abby.

Active in the Ivanrest Christian Reformed Church, Bishop also spent 13 years watching, coaching and umpiring in the Grandville Little League.

"Both boys stopped playing when they were 16, so I've been away from baseball since 1999 and I miss it still," Bishop said. "I might start umpiring again next year, Lord willing."

The Bishops call Grandville home, and Randy says, "We're pretty much middle-of-the-road middle America. Not an overwhelmingly exciting life."

One, however, that suits the "quiet" manager just fine.

CHAPTER 10

Post-Championship Years

Veteran Spartan

O nly one member of the current MSU basketball staff was employed at the time the 1979 team won the NCAA title—secretary Lori Soderberg.

Lori graduated from Lansing Everett High School the year Earvin Johnson was a sophomore. She was not a big basketball fan and only saw several of the Vikings' games.

Lori took a secretarial job at MSU in the Horticulture Department, but soon transferred to athletics, where she worked for then baseball coach Danny Litwhiler. At the time, she was dating the cousin of Chris Smith, who was the basketball secretary to former coach Gus Ganakas. When Gus was removed from his coaching post, Chris stayed on for six months more to help Jud Heathcote in the transition period.

Chris knew Lori and suggested she apply for the basketball job. She interviewed for it and began in December of 1976. She is still on the staff as Tom Izzo's secretary, although her job requirements are far more involved today than they were 25 years ago.

"Jud scared me at times, but he never got angry with me like he did with the assistant coaches," she recalls with a smile. "He mellowed out over the years."

Back in 1979, being young and inexperienced, her job wasn't as complicated as it is today. She has her own impressive office at the Breslin Center today located adjacent to Izzo's. And she still visits regularly with the 1979 players.

"Mike Longaker dropped by when he adopted his baby at Sparrow Hospital," she recalls. "Rob Gonzalez calls from time to time. Terry Donnelly always stops in when he's here once a year and occasionally he goes on road trips today.

"Of course, I always see Greg Kelser during the season because of all his broadcast work. And I see Earvin when he's in town and stops by."

She didn't know much about MSU basketball when she landed her job.

"I only knew about the players' walkout when Gus was the coach in 1976," Lori said.

Retirement plans?

"I still have kids in school. I can't retire yet."

Those who know Lori Soderberg respect her temperament and organizational skills in a demanding job today. And she was appreciated greatly by both Jud and Tom.

During one postseason banquet, Jud made a point to thank his secretary.

"She really does a great job," he deadpanned. "I don't know where she is out there in the audience—she's probably back at the bar someplace."

Mutual Support

D uring the Spartans' run to the 2000 NCAA championship, members of the 1979 team helped along the way.

Greg Kelser broadcast a number of games on television, and he spoke with several players, offering encouragement through the course of the season.

The Spartans struggled at one point early in the Big Ten schedule when Earvin Johnson asked to speak with Mateen Cleaves.

"Earvin told Mateen to smile and have fun," coach Tom Izzo recalls. "He thought we were playing tight. He thought we needed to ease the pressure. He helped a great deal, because Mateen seemed to smile for the rest of the season out on the court."

1979 guard Terry Donnelly visited the Spartans during their regional round in St. Louis. Donnelly followed the 2000 season closely on television, and he has always tried to remain close to Tom Izzo's program.

Mike Brkovich visited during the 2000 season, and Ron Charles also attended a game in the Breslin Center.

Comparisons

I f the 1979 team played the 2000 team, which of the Spartans' national championship units would have won?

"The 1979 team would have won," Tom Izzo says. "They were more physical, and of course, they had Earvin. They had six superb players, and our team was probably better from our first player through number nine. We would have made it an interesting game, though, and Mateen Cleaves would have tried to find a way that the 2000 team could win too.

"Containing Earvin would have been difficult, and we would have faced matchup problems," Izzo adds. "The '79 team's fast break was lethal. Earvin rebounded so well and then ran the break

Earvin Johnson, MVP of the 1979 Final Four, and Terry Donnelly, the Spartans' Most Improved Player in 1978-79, share a laugh on the end of Michigan State's bench after their careers were complete. *Photo courtesy of MSU Sports Information*

so quickly. Their matchup zone would also have given us problems."

The two teams' defenses differed greatly. The '79 team almost exclusively used a matchup zone while Izzo's 2000 unit was a man-to-man club. Izzo says different personnel made the different defenses the most beneficial to each group.

Anything similar?

"Both teams had terrific fast breaks," Izzo says. "And they both had incredible winners. Earvin put winning above any personal satisfaction. And Mateen was all about winning. There aren't ten players in America like Earvin and Mateen anymore."

So what are Izzo's memories of that special victory over Indiana State?

"Terry Donnelly had the good game and Earvin kept finding him," Izzo said. "Ron Charles was a good support player that night and, of course, Kelser had a big game off Earvin's passes. They had such good fun whenever they played and it sure did show.

"What also impresses me about the '79 team is how they all come back for the reunions together. They have always had a sense of team about them."

Another Prediction

Gus Ganakas, head coach from 1969 through 1976, offers his thoughts on a matchup of the '79 team versus the 2000 team:

"Who would we make the favorite, the '79 team by about six points?" Gus laughs. "That sounds pretty close. It's difficult to say who would actually win. It would be pretty close."

Gus broadcast ten games on television for the 1979 team. And he called all the games on radio for the 2000 team. So he saw them both up close and personal. Gregory Kelser was Gus's recruit out of Detroit Henry Ford High School and played for him his freshman year before Ganakas was reassigned in the athletic department.

A Magical Assessment

If the 1979 team played the 2000 team—at their peak— who would win? Surely you don't think Earvin Johnson would pick Tom Izzo's guys, do you?

Earvin Johnson had a great deal of interest in the 2000 team's title run. He spoke with the players, especially Mateen Cleaves, frequently through that season. He was in Indianapolis for the Final Four and helped cut down the nets. He loved the 2000 team's heart and fortitude. But naturally, Earvin thinks his '79 Spartans would have won a mythical matchup.

"We were hard to defend," Earvin said. "We played many guys out of position and we had guys who could play several positions well. We knew each other's moves inside and out.

"Our team had more playmakers."

Earvin rattles off the names of the key players. He loved Terry Donnelly's pure shooting touch, especially in clutch situations. Earvin well remembers Donnelly's perfect five-for-five shooting night in Salt Lake City in the final game against Indiana State. He mentions Mike Brkovich in the same breath.

Earvin always has sung the praise of Greg Kelser's talent and will remind one and all about his long NBA career as well as that of Jay Vincent. Earvin likes to describe Jay as an atypical center because of his many offensive moves underneath and away from the basket. Ron Charles was a key role player and rebounder. And, of course, there was Earvin's presence to unify the entire package.

Nostalgic Road Trip

The instructions were implicit. Meet at the M-DOT building at Capitol City Airport, 3 p.m. sharp, Friday, September 27, 2002. The plane would leave promptly at 3:15 and return approximately twelve hours later.

That was the word from trip coordinator Tom Izzo, who organized a party of seven to head to Springfield, Massachusetts and that night's Basketball Hall of Fame induction ceremonies featuring Earvin Johnson. Izzo had access to private airplanes, and this was an occasion he thought he should attend and wanted to make it special for Earvin's two coaches in high school and college.

Jud Heathcote and wife Bev would be on the plane, and so would George Fox and wife Theresa. MSU basketball publicist Matt Larsen would also be aboard. And, of course, Lupe Izzo would be there with Tom.

To make the trip the Heathcotes would have to return to Michigan from their Spokane, Washington home for the second time in two weeks. They attended the Notre Dame game after Jud spoke at a retirement party for Cooley Law School founder Tom Brennan, Sr., two nights earlier. The two were friends from Walnut Hills Country Club days.

So on September 26, Jud and Bev flew back to Michigan to be on the flight to the hall of fame. The Foxes were especially elated to be invited because they otherwise might not have made the trip.

Despite the late return, in the middle of the night, Tom Izzo was back on campus bright and early Saturday morning to make the pre-football game rounds. And Jud and Bev were in their press box booth by the 1 p.m. kickoff, tired but still awestruck by the marvelous day they had enjoyed 24 hours earlier.

Today's Game

If you listen to Earvin Johnson, college basketball is in trouble today.

"All these high school players—they think they're ready for the NBA. Look how many sit on the bench with limited skills because they didn't develop in college," Earvin said.

Earvin believes many players of this generation, 25 years removed from the '79 Spartans, don't have nearly the dedication the players on his team exhibited.

He coached 16 games at the end of one Lakers season and had enough of that. His team lost ten in a row at one stretch, but Earvin didn't want to put up with players' cell phones at practice and a lack of commitment—something Earvin had in abundance.

"When I played at Michigan State, every guy was here during the summer playing pickup games together," Earvin recalled. "We would play four-on-four games from 8 p.m. to midnight. Then after a short break, we'd play several more hours until two or three o'clock in the morning.

"We loved each other and we loved to play. UCLA's team last year assembled to play one month before the season began, and that's why they are where they are today. We were in the gym every night—we truly were magical Spartans!"

Johnson has invited numerous NBA wannabe college players to work out with him privately, including former Spartan Marcus Taylor. What they gave up by leaving college early, Earvin has tried to make up by providing his own tips from his knowledge and experience.

"I helped Pig Miller [former Spartan] get into the NBA, and I hope I can help Marcus," Earvin said.

Like most others, Earvin believes most college underclassmen declare too early for the NBA draft because the lure of the money is so great. He knew he wasn't ready to become a professional star after his freshman year at Michigan State. And when he did join the Lakers, he immediately helped lead them to the 1980 NBA championship.

A Magical Name

The story has been well documented over the years of how Earvin Johnson became Magic Johnson—and the world truly knows this basketball celebrity as Magic Johnson. The impact of that name has not been lost on its owner.

"My life has truly been different because of that nickname," Earvin said.

"Worldwide, I'm known as 'Magic.' Kids only know me as 'Magic.' Only in Lansing do people call me Earvin.

"It's catchy. Everybody in sports is trying to get a nickname because it sells. And the name Magic still sells."

Johnson has used the name in business extensively beyond his playing career. Today the world has the Magic Theatres. Earvin is the only franchisee of TGI Fridays to have his nickname on the front end of the restaurants he owns. The 24-hour Magic Johnson Fitness Centers have been organized along with other business holdings.

Earvin knew early on that he needed sole ownership of the name Magic. He owns the copyright to it worldwide.

Another Vincent in Green and White

J ayson Vincent bears a striking facial resemblance to his father, Jay Vincent, the fifth leading scorer in Michigan State history.

He's also following the family tradition of wearing the green and white, just like his father and uncle, Sam Vincent, the sixth leading scorer in Spartan annals.

The 6'4", 210-pound guard is a sophomore walk-on for MSU basketball team.

"He's way tougher than I was," said the proud father. "If I had the dedication that he has, I'd have been an All-Star 10 or 12 times. He really works at it."

Jayson, who averaged 19 points and nine rebounds a game as a senior power forward at Mason High, missed the 2001-02 season with a broken ankle.

CHAPTER 11

Spartan Nuggets

Fitting Climax to NBA Career

Jay Vincent couldn't have scripted it any better.

The former Lansing Eastern and Michigan State great finished his NBA career playing with the Los Angeles Lakers and former rival, teammate and close friend, Earvin "Magic" Johnson.

The season was 1989-90 AKAJ (After Kareem Abdul-Jabbar), and the Lakers posted the best record in basketball at 63-19. However, they were ousted in the first round of the NBA playoffs by the Phoenix Suns.

"To finish my NBA career with Earvin was just perfect," Vincent said. "We started being friends back in grade school, and played many games together and against each other.

"It was kind of nice, two guys from Lansing playing in the NBA together. I had a successful career and he had an enormous one."

Vincent never really thought about playing in the NBA until after Gregory Kelser and Johnson had signed their pro contracts.

"When they came driving onto campus in their fancy cars, that's when I began thinking about it," Vincent said. "Kelser was a scorer, and I felt I could score, too."

Vincent led the Big Ten in scoring as a junior and senior and was a first-round pick of the Dallas Mavericks.

It took an injury to former DePaul star Mark Aguirre to help launch Vincent's NBA career. When Aguirre was sidelined, Jay stepped in and averaged 27.3 points per game the rest of the season.

He was named to the All-Rookie first team and finished second in balloting for Rookie of the Year to Isiah Thomas of the Detroit Pistons.

Vincent spent his first five years with Dallas before going to Washington for a year, Denver for two and one-half years, and one with the Lakers.

The 6'8" Vincent ended his pro career in Italy in 1993 when he tore his right Achilles tendon. He played for Milan.

"Playing in Italy was a good experience, but it was kind of scary for me," Vincent said. "I didn't know anybody in a strange country, but I did learn some Italian and I got to know the city of Milan very well."

Comments Still Linger

Try as he might, Jay Vincent has never quite been able to get out of his mind something that Jud Heathcote said during his senior season at Michigan State.

"He said that I was the best player in the Big Ten with the basketball, and the worst without it," Vincent said. "That bothered me, because I was trying to make it in the pros, and it came back to haunt me.

"That came up when I was being interviewed by pro teams before the draft. I've got nothing against Coach Heathcote, and I've forgiven him for saying it, but it lingered on for a long time."

Vincent, who led the Big Ten in scoring twice, always wondered if Heathcote's comments cost him when the 1981 NBA draft was held.

"I was projected to go as high as the top 10 but wasn't picked until the 19th by Dallas," Vincent said.

Vincent's stoic play on the floor could also have been a factor.

"I always kept my emotions under control," Vincent said. "I was kind of like the quiet assassin, and that confused people. It's hard to read quiet and unemotional people."

Vincent's NBA Career Almost Stalled Early

Jay Vincent was the first pick of the second round of the 1981 NBA draft by the Dallas Mavericks. However, he nearly didn't make it out of training camp.

Dallas coach Dick Motta, a friend of Jud Heathcote's when Motta was at Weber State, called Jud and said he was going to cut Vincent.

Motta told Jud that Jay was overweight and couldn't run or jump.

"I told Motta that he should look at what Jay could do," Heathcote said. "He had great hands, was a splendid passer and could hit that short- to mid-range jumper."

Motta kept Vincent, and when Mark Aguirre injured his ankle, Jay moved into the starting lineup. He averaged 21.4 points per game and made the NBA All-Rookie team.

"Motta called me after the season and told me that it was a good thing he listened to me, because they had a good year and he ended up being named 'Coach of the Year' in the NBA," Heathcote said.

Jay played nine years in the NBA for six teams and averaged in twin figures seven of those seasons. For his career, Vincent averaged 15.2 points, 5.5 rebounds and 2.0 assists per game.

BoBo Never Concerned About Earvin

Few people knew Earvin Johnson better in college than Ron "Bobo" Charles. They practiced, partied, and roomed together on the road for two years.

Many people thought the worst when Earvin contracted HIV, but not Bobo.

"When I first heard about it, I said he's going to live a long life," Charles recalled. "There's just something about him ... something magical."

Bobo still sees Earvin whenever he comes to Atlanta, and hopes to get him to go to St. Croix in the Virgin Islands when Charles's old Central High dedicates the gymnasium in his honor.

"But he's so busy that he's hard to pin down," Charles said.

Charles used to work out regularly with Terry Donnelly at Georgia Tech when Donnelly still lived in Atlanta, and he visits often with Gregory Kelser.

"I got to see a lot of the guys at the Final Fours in Tampa and Minneapolis, and I was hoping the Spartans would make it in 2002 here in Atlanta, but it didn't work out," he said. "I still follow Michigan State on a regular basis and get back as often as I can.

"I'm proud of the job Tom Izzo has done with that program."

Please Shoot!

Rarely do you have a basketball player come along with a pure stroke who is reluctant to shoot.

Mike Brkovich was one of those guys.

"Mike never had the confidence he needed with the shot he had," Spartans head coach Jud Heathcote said. "Brk worked hard at his game and would always ask me to help him with his shot after practice.

Mike Brkovich had many great moments for Michigan State during his career. The 6'4" guard from Windsor, Ontario is shown dunking in Michigan State's 85-61 thrashing of Kansas in Jenison Field House. *Photo courtesy of MSU Sports Information*

"He'd make 10 in a row and then miss one, and say 'See, I just don't know what's wrong.'"

In the two years after Earvin Johnson and Gregory Kelser took off for the NBA, Michigan State needed Brkovich to be an offensive weapon, but he didn't have the shooter's mentality.

"He'd miss one or two shots in a row, and he'd run by the bench and tell me that somebody else needed to shoot because he was off," Heathcote said. "We didn't have too many other options."

15 Years Before the Ring Fit

For 15 years, Rick Kaye had a beautiful NCAA championship ring ... one that didn't fit.

"I broke my ring finger on my right hand just before we had the ring presentation," said Kaye, a sophomore forward on MSU's 1979 NCAA Championship squad. "The ring never fit, so I just kept it locked up."

It stayed that way until 1994 when Kaye went to a jeweler looking for another ring ... one for his wedding.

"I talked with the jeweler and he convinced me to get it resized," Kaye said. "It was a risk, because there was a chance the green on the ring could be ruined."

All worked out well, and now the ring's always on his right hand.

"Once people find out that I played on Michigan State's championship team, they always want to see my ring," Kaye said. "And they also want to know what it was like playing with Earvin Johnson."

So, how was it playing with Magic?

"It was an absolute thrill," said Kaye. "He was an incredible competitor who took his game to the next level and took the whole team with him.

MSU forward Rick Kaye wasn't able to wear his 1979 NCAA championship ring for 15 years because of a broken finger. He finally had it resized when at a jewelry store to buy a wedding ring. *Photo courtesy of MSU Sports Information*

"Earvin always felt that the pass was more important than the basket. However, he would do what it took to win—rebound, score, get a steal, whatever."

Kaye was there one time, however, when Earvin's monstrous skills weren't enough.

It was in 1976 in the Class A semis when Kaye's Detroit Catholic Central team eliminated Johnson's Lansing Everett team en route to the state title.

"Earvin always kids me about that game," Kaye said. "And Everett coach George Fox always brings it up whenever I see him."

Everett did gain a margin of revenge the following year by winning the state crown after Catholic Central was ousted in the semis by Birmingham Brother Rice.

Memorable Moments in Rose Arena

If there's any basketball arena in the world I've seen more games in than Jenison Field House, it would have to be Central Michigan University's Rose Arena.

I'm in my 22nd year as the sports information director at CMU, and I figure I've seen more than 500 games played in the 5,200-seat arena.

I went to only one game at Rose before moving to Mount Pleasant, and it was a memorable one involving Michigan State.

It was Jud Heathcote's first game as the Spartans coach in 1976, and the Chippewas pulled a major upset, 81-76, before an overflow crowd.

I covered the game for *The State Journal*, and I remember the stands were jammed and people were hanging over the railings at all four corners.

Following the game, Heathcote vowed, "I'll never play there again."

And, he didn't.

One play that stands out in the game involved Gregory Kelser, MSU's gravity-defying leaper. On a breakaway early in the game, Kelser did a split-legged flying dunk over future NBA journeyman Ben Poquette, nearly clearing the 6'9" center.

The dunk had just been reinstated that year, and Kelser's slam took everyone quite off guard. In fact, the place went dead silent for a moment before erupting into a thunderous ovation.

A couple of years later, a beak-nosed, blond-haired lad from Indiana State named Larry Bird also wowed the Rose crowd.

CMU head coach Dick Parfitt remembers clearly an episode before the game during warmups.

"I was intently watching our guys go through warmups when all of a sudden our crowd erupted with a thunderous cheer," Parfitt recalled.

He looked around and couldn't see the reason for the commotion. Finally, he asked his assistant coach Dave Ginsberg what all the noise was about.

"Bird just missed," Ginsberg said.

"I had been out there for at least five minutes, and that was his first miss," Parfitt said. "Our fans cheered for every miss, and they cheered only five times during the entire warmup."

He didn't miss much during the game, either, as he set an arena record with 45 points.

—*Fred Stabley Jr.*

Not the Class It Could Have Been

Most teams reap the benefits of winning an NCAA basketball championship by having a banner recruiting class.

Not Michigan State!

Because it took so long for Earvin Johnson to decide to turn professional following the NCAA title in 1979, the Spartans came up short in the recruiting battles.

"We lost four or five players who would have come if Earvin had stayed, and we lost players who would have come had they known Earvin was leaving," Heathcote said. "So it didn't turn out to be the class we had hoped."

One of those who was going to become a Spartan had Magic stayed was 6'9" Sidney Green, who ended up at UNLV and had a fine NBA career. Two more who considered MSU were 7'4" Ralph Sampson (he went to Virginia) and 6'11" Granville Waiters (Ohio State).

Why did it take Magic so long to announce?

"First of all, I wanted to enjoy the championship as much as I could," Earvin said. "And then, I had to go to this banquet and that, and before you knew it, two weeks had gone by.

"Also I went out to Los Angeles to talk with the Lakers. Once I saw The Forum, that was it."

Heathcote's incoming class for 1979-80 was made up of 6'7" forward Derek Perry (River Rouge), 6'8" forward Evaristo Perez (Orchard Lake St. Mary), 6'5" guard Herb Bostic (Royal Oak Shrine), and 6'6" forward Kurt James (Oakland Community College). Two transfers who sat out the 1978-79 campaign would also become eligible for the following season—6'10" Steve Bates (Arkansas) and 6'2" Kevin Smith (Detroit).

Media Moments

Lynn Henning of the *Lansing State Journal* had more than one go-around with Jud Heathcote while covering the Spartans, but 25 years later those memories produce mostly laughs.

"Jud is and always will be a great friend," Lynn says. "He has done some very nice things for me over the years even though we struggled at times during the Spartans' two great seasons in 1978 and 1979.

"My uncle asked me if I could get Jud to come speak to his small group in the spring of 1977. This was while he was recruiting Earvin Johnson. He wanted to recruit at the Detroit

Catholic League playoffs, but he remembered he had made a commitment to me and he honored it that night.

"This wasn't any big group, either—20 guys, maybe, and Jud was at his best. He never asked if he would get paid either.

"Another time, just a couple of years ago, I asked him if he could call a pair of kids who'd been suspended for the season from the basketball team at Saline High School. These were 16-year-olds and they'd made a mistake, but they weren't bad kids. But they were going to miss basketball for the entire winter. So Jud called these kids and left a pep talk on their machine when no one answered. It did a tremendous amount of good for them, and frankly, they were psychologically saved. All because of Jud.

"I remember I told him I was leaving Lansing and going to Detroit to work for the *News* shortly after the '79 season ended. He told me I wasn't going far enough."

On the Move with the Spartans

Since coming to Central Michigan University in 1982 as the sports information director, I've often been asked by people, "What's the best and worst thing about your job?"

I've been giving the same answer now for more than 36 years, all the way back to my first days at *The State Journal* in 1967. It's the travel.

On one hand, you love it because of all the wonderful and unique places you get to go to. On the other, you're away from your family way too often.

For instance, covering the 1978-79 Spartans took me to 11 different states. We were as far west as Oregon and as far east as North Carolina.

We spent many days in airports, chasing the Spartans around the country, and logged many more hours driving throughout the Midwest following the Spartan fortunes at Big Ten venues.

We also got quite a variety in music, going from the Grand Ole Opry in Nashville one week and to a Mormon Tabernacle Choir performance in Salt Lake City two weeks later.

By the way, I've been to 42 states in my 21 years at CMU.

—Fred Stabley Jr.

Investigation

The recruitment of Earvin Johnson drew interest from NCAA enforcement officers. Whichever school ended up with the Lansing high school star was almost certain to be investigated. The NCAA wanted to know if anyone made any illegal offers to either Earvin, his family or to his coach George Fox.

Somehow, the NCAA learned that Fox and his Everett assistant, Pat Holland, had been invited to travel with the MSU team to the Final Four in Salt Lake City. Jud and George had become good friends. Jud told Fox and Holland, "You guys are the head of the 'Hosting Committee.' Their trip to the Final Four obviously had nothing to do with MSU landing Earvin Johnson.

Fox and Holland loved the experience like all of the MSU fans did. They put a case of beer in their hotel room for the week and invited various friends up to enjoy the tournament spectacle.

The next summer, two NCAA investigators grilled Fox over the entire experience at a hotel across the street from Lansing's Frandor Shopping Center. Fox convinced them that he had worked in the summers at MSU since 1957 and his involvement with the MSU team had absolutely nothing to do with whom Earvin Johnson would play for as a collegian. The matter ended with that meeting.

CHAPTER 12

Magic Moments

Magic Joins the Hall of Fame

I never expected it to affect me the way it did when Earvin Johnson was inducted into the Basketball Hall of Fame.

I sat there in Section 25, Row F of the Springfield Civic Center on Friday, September 27, 2002, virtually spellbound.

I was as proud as a peacock of the Magic man when he took his place among the elite in basketball … a tear or two welling in my eyes.

I wasn't there when "EJ the DJ," as he liked to be called in his early days (he once wanted to be a disc jockey), first started playing basketball.

But I was there in early December of 1974 when he played his first game for Lansing Everett High–a narrow win at Holt High.

I was there when Earvin won the Class A state championship in 1977, and I was courtside at the Special Events Center in Salt Lake City when the Spartans won the NCAA title in 1979. To say that Earvin "Magic" Johnson has been a big part of my life would be akin to saying that Earvin could pass the basketball.

It all came back to me that evening at the Hall of Fame ceremonies, where Who's Who in basketball were assembled—legends like Larry Bird, Lou Carnesecca, Bob Cousy, Chuck Daly, Marques Haynes, Ray Meyer, Bob Pettit and Willis Reed, to name a few.

As usual, though, Earvin was the hit of the show.

He went in with coaching greats Larry Brown, Lute Olson and Kay Yow, the Harlem Globetrotters and the late Drazen Petrovic.

But it seemed as though most of them came to cheer on the pride of Lansing.

In fact, a busload of Earvin's biggest fans came to Springfield, Mass., for the big event. Tom Izzo (MSU's current coach) and Jud Heathcote (Earvin's coach at MSU) along with George Fox (his Lansing Everett mentor) and their wives flew there on a private plane.

What has happened to that remarkable young man with the ear-to-ear smile and the big Afro since our paths first crossed in 1974 has been truly incredible.

Often considered one of the top five basketball players of all time, Earvin is now a wealthy businessman, well spoken and philanthropic. He carries himself with grace and has his family as a top priority. He credits his parents, Christine and Earvin Sr., with making him the person he is today, and with Cookie for being "a wife, mother and best friend all at the same time."

He also understands he's a very lucky man in more ways than one.

"I have to thank God," he said to begin his induction speech. "Eleven years ago, I didn't know if I would be here to accept this award."

Magic was diagnosed with the HIV virus in 1991, the virus that causes AIDS. He still has no AIDS symptoms and has been told by his doctors that the HIV virus is "asleep."

I, for one, along with his millions of fans worldwide, hope and pray that it remains "asleep" for a long time to come.

He's one of a kind, and I feel blessed to have known him for all of these years.

—*Fred Stabley Jr.*

Magic Picked Bird

Earvin Johnson could have picked any number of basketball greats to present him for induction into the Basketball Hall of Fame in 2002.

Who ever would have guessed the Magic Man would pick Larry Bird?

Once archrivals, the two have become fast friends, building a lasting relationship based on respect and admiration.

Bird told a story to the Hall of Fame crowd in Springfield, Mass.

"I came back from an All-Star game, and I told my brother that I saw the best basketball player I'm ever going to see in my life," Bird said of Earvin. "After the NCAA championship game, my brother came up and said, 'Yea, he's a lot better than you.'"

The two reveled in beating each other on the floor ever since MSU dumped Indiana State in the 1979 NCAA finals.

The rivalry continued in the pros as the Bird-led Boston Celtics and the Johnson-led Los Angeles Lakers dominated the NBA throughout the 1980s. The two superstars helped rejuvenate a pro game that seemingly had marked time for years.

Larry and Earvin became friends in the mid-1980s while spending time together filming TV commercials. Despite opposite backgrounds (Bird grew up in rural French Lick, Ind., and Johnson was a city kid from Lansing), the two found a common bond in a love for basketball, the willingness to outwork anyone, and the thrill of making a great pass.

"Once we stepped on the court, we were enemies," Bird said. "But the great thing about the relationship is that off the floor we were friends."

Each credits the other for making him better.

"I wouldn't be here if there was no Larry Bird," Magic said. "I'd go to the gym and stay six hours because I knew Larry would be there, too. He was the person driving me. I always checked the box scores. I always knew he'd be shooting thousands of shots each day. I just had to keep up."

Bird agreed.

"I worked hard every day for one reason," Bird said. "I was always trying to beat Earvin and those damn Lakers. He definitely made my game better."

Bird recalled sitting in the bus outside the Forum after a rare Celtics win at the Lakers' home court.

"I saw Earvin come out of the Forum and head to his car," Bird said. "I could see the pain on his face and the look in his eye. He was a beaten man.

"And I said to myself, 'Suffer, baby, suffer.' I knew that he was going to go home without dinner and sit in the dark for a couple of hours. I know. I'd been there myself."

Bird went on to say that Earvin was one of the two greatest ever to play the game, Michael Jordan being the other.

"I wanted to speak from the heart tonight," Bird said, in his closing remarks. "But he broke my heart too many times that I didn't have any left."

Fellow inductee Larry Brown also had kind words for Johnson.

"I wish every kid out there would recognize how unselfishly he played," Brown said. "He revolutionized the game for everyone. Underneath that smile was a fierce competitor."

The Harlem Globetrotters, known for their showmanship and incredible passes, also were inducted that evening. After a film featuring the Globetrotters and their crowd-pleasing antics, emcee Ahmad Rashad looked at Earvin in the front row and said, "You know you stole some of that stuff, don't you?"

Johnson's heartfelt admiration of Bird was obvious, too.

"It was tremendous playing against you," Johnson said to Bird during his induction speech. "Thank God I got to know you not just as Larry Bird the basketball player but Larry Bird the person."

Always ready for some competition, though, Earvin then suggested that Bird and he get together for another game—this time, checkers.

"Or we could play a game of P-I-G," he joked. "I don't think we could make it through a game of H-O-R-S-E."

You Can Count on Jud

It was early on a summer morning after Earvin Johnson's first year in the NBA, and Magic was shooting baskets by himself in Jenison Field House.

He heard a familiar voice bellow from the stands ... Jud Heathcote. As usual, Jud was kidding Earvin about one thing or another.

"We talked for a while and Jud said he'd meet me every day if I wanted to work on my shooting," Johnson said. "So we met for four straight weeks at 10 a.m., and we did it for a number of summers after that.

"That's the kind of guy Jud was. I'm glad I didn't go to Michigan because I wouldn't have gotten any better."

With Jud you had no choice.

"Jud's way of showing he loved you was picking on you," Earvin said. "I can't tell you how many times I heard him holler, 'I want a guard, not garbage.' He was a perfectionist, and you couldn't help but get your talent perfected under him.

"I think the reason we got along was because we were so much alike. I hated to lose and so did he.

"The man was a winner. He was a successful coach who cared about his players. He battled for his players."

The ever-intense Jud Heathcote was a great teacher who spent countless hours during the summer working on Earvin Johnson's outside shot after Magic's career at Michigan State was over. *Photo courtesy of MSU Sports Information*

Magic Excels in Business

E arvin Johnson has always been a big dreamer.
When cleaning the offices of Lansing businessmen Greg Eaton and Joel Ferguson as a teenager, he'd often plop down in one of their chairs, put his feet up on the desk and dream about being successful one day in business himself.

"Greg and Joe were two guys I looked up to and idolized as businessmen," Earvin said. "I was always curious. I would ask people in business how they did this and how they got to where they were."

But not even could Magic have dreamed he'd have the success in the business world that he's had.

"I leveraged the nickname 'Magic' and my basketball career," Earvin said.

"I took advantage of every opportunity I had. Still, I'm surprised with my good fortune in business."

Earvin is the CEO of Magic Johnson Enterprises and employs more than 3,000 people in his various enterprises.

Included in his holdings are: 57 Starbucks (plans call for more than 100 in a couple of years); a 47-store Fatburger fast-food chain; TGI Friday restaurants that bear his name; a music label; 24-hour fitness centers; six movie theatres; six malls; a movie called *Brown Sugar*; and part ownership in the Class A Dayton Ranger baseball team.

What kind of CEO is Magic? Definitely hands-on.

"I'm on the road more than 150 days each year because of business," Earvin said. "People don't realize how involved I am."

As one can see, Earvin is still a competitor … only this time he's using his skills and drive to succeed in the business world.

Cookie Did Her Own "Recruiting"

Earvin Johnson was used to being "recruited." Michigan State beat out hordes of suitors for Magic's services out of high school, and the NBA's Kansas City Kings did their best to "recruit" Earvin after his freshman season at MSU.

The Los Angeles Lakers finally convinced Magic to turn pro the following season during a visit to the West Coast.

Throughout most of this time, there was another persistent "recruiter" chasing Earvin. Her given name was Earleatha Kelly, but ever since she was a child her mother called her "Cookie."

She was Earvin's girlfriend from the winter of 1978 through most of his college and professional career. Twice they were engaged, and twice Earvin broke it off.

"I was married to basketball, and I didn't know if she could understand what I was going through," Magic said. "I was a moody, crazy person during the season."

Cookie was working in Toledo in 1990 when she told Earvin she couldn't take it anymore. She just had to be with him.

"I'd never had her with me, but she was determined this time," Earvin recalled.

On her own, Cookie flew to Los Angeles on a Monday, had three job interviews on a Tuesday, and had three jobs offers to wade through on Wednesday.

"She spent the whole year with me and convinced me she could handle my crazy moods," Earvin said. "It was great having her with me—I always had somebody to talk to."

On September 14, 1991, the two were married in Lansing's Union Missionary Baptist Church.

Less than six weeks later, Earvin's world crumbled around him. On October 25, he was told that he had HIV, the virus that leads to AIDS.

When Earvin needed her the most, Cookie responded with strength, spirituality, understanding, and love.

"First of all, she stayed with me," Earvin said. "Second, she went with me to the doctors to know what she could do as a wife to help me.

"And, finally, she booted me out of the house. She told me that I was driving her crazy just moping around the house. She told me to get on with my life and start working out and going to the office again.

"She told me to be 'Earvin.'"

Earvin took her advice and hasn't looked back.

"Cookie is my best friend and a great mother," said Earvin. "She's my heart … I love her."

Cookie also got Earvin involved in church again, something that he's enjoyed immensely.

"She's been a blessing to me," Earvin said.

Stats Sheets

Part of the postgame routine after every Michigan State basketball game is for a runner to bring numerous copies of the statistics to the dressing room. All of the players get a copy along with coaches, and there are enough to go around for everyone interested.

The players gobbled them up on a regular basis in 1979 to see how many rebounds they snared, shots they took, etc.

One guy never took a stats sheet—Earvin Johnson.

"Earvin only cared about winning," Jud Heathcote recalls. "When the players asked him if he'd like a copy, he always said he'd just check the papers the next day. The only stat he truly cared about was simply winning."

The Nickname...
My Version

When a story gets retold by people over a period of time, different versions tend to emerge. In the case of Earvin Johnson becoming Magic Johnson, most all of the accounts I have seen are quite similar.

While Fred Stabley Jr. covered high school games directly, my workload prohibited my leaving the studio most nights. I had to prepare late-night sportscasts from my office while photographers alone would shoot game clips. Hence, I didn't get to see Earvin Johnson play in person for the first few games at Everett High School.

Fred indeed did call me at my office one night to sound me out on calling him "Magic," and after a few seconds, I replied that I thought the name was too corny. "It'll never last," I told him assuredly. I couldn't believe some tenth grader possessed the skills worthy of such a name.

Fred has always believed that if he didn't nickname Earvin "Magic," then someone else would have. I'm not so sure. Early in Earvin's sophomore season, Fred covered a game in which Earvin scored 36 points to go with 18 rebounds, 16 assists and ten steals. That's a quadruple double by today's parlance—not too bad! And that performance against Jackson Parkside High School convinced Fred that it was time to test his nickname out on me.

If my recommendation against the name "Magic" did nothing else, it delayed the moniker from getting into the newspaper. Fred tried it out around his office, but it wasn't until a month later that the name Earvin "Magic" Johnson found its way into print after another superb performance against Parkside, this time in Jackson.

Lakers coach Pat Riley never liked the nickname because it conjured up an image, he felt, that "sounded like a player who didn't work hard in practice."

"The name became a challenge," Earvin said in his autobiograhy, *My Life*, "and I love challenges. To me, being known as Magic Johnson has always been an honor and a great motivator. I've spent the rest of my career trying to live up to it."

I've often wondered over the years how Earvin's life might have been different had he not been known as Magic Johnson. Very few NBA fans ever referred to him as Earvin. The name Magic was perfect for marketing purposes, and, of course, with Earvin's personality the potential for growth beyond basketball was enormous.

His parents were never overly fond of the name, particularly his mother, who is quite religious. She felt such a term implied that her son could do things humans otherwise could not do. As a basketball player such an implied term was clearly accurate!

I was never comfortable calling him Magic over all these years—I always told him that was a fan's salutation. I met him as Earvin and I've known him as Earvin and that's what I've always called him. He learned to accept people around the world referring to him as Magic and it never affected him at all.

It is arguably the most famous nickname in sports. And just think, my retort to Fred that night on the phone was "How about

'The Franchise?'" Even though he was clearly a franchise player for his entire sport, there was no "magic" in that name whatsoever!

—Tim Staudt

Magic's Impact

So what would Michigan State be like had Earvin Johnson played down the road in Ann Arbor during his college days? What effect would his absence have had on the school? Twenty-five years later, what influence does Earvin Johnson still have on the university? All good questions—and one person's perspective:

At the time Earvin announced he'd become a Spartan, the school's athletic fortunes, especially basketball, clearly needed a shot in the arm. Attendance in Jenison Field House was down. Jud Heathcote's first season produced a mere 10-17 record, so without Earvin's recruitment, fans had no reason to expect a brighter future.

The football program was on NCAA probation. In the late '70s, Michigan was a football powerhouse under legendary coach Bo Schembechler, and the Wolverine basketball teams regularly had their way with the Spartans. Earvin's announcement changed much of the perceptions that fans had about the two schools.

Suddenly, Michigan State was in the national limelight. Tickets were tough to obtain, just as they were for Everett High School games the previous three years. Jud Heathcote became more quotable. His sense of humor received more exposure.

Earvin alone did not get the Breslin Center built, but he clearly played a key role. The new interest in MSU basketball meant the school would make a move upward in its commitment and facilities. Jenison Field House was Earvin's home, but it had outlived its usefulness if the Spartan program was to continue to grow. And the momentum in basketball made the difficult financial decision of committing $43 million to the new arena much more acceptable to all concerned.

One of the key plays in the NCAA championship game was this dunk by Earvin Johnson and a flagrant foul called for undercutting on Bobby Heaton (30) that led to a four-point play and a 61-50 Spartan lead. *Photo courtesy of MSU Sports Information*

The 1979 NCAA title game still holds the all-time record for highest television ratings of a college basketball tournament game. And the millions of people watching became well aware of Michigan State University. Financial contributions increased, and so did enrollment requests from high school seniors.

Earvin never did graduate. Frankly, there just wasn't time. His life was totally consumed by his entrance into the NBA after that title game in Salt Lake City.

Some at Michigan State wish he would have found the time to earn a degree, and some are critical that he has not made more of a financial commitment to the school.

Others, like current MSU head coach Tom Izzo, are well satisfied with Earvin's help over the years.

"Earvin has been tremendous to us," Izzo said. "He has helped us recruit and done anything I've ever asked him to do. He speaks to our players and he attended all of the Final Fours. He gave us the exhibition games for a small fee."

Earvin loves college football and regularly follows the gridiron Spartans. He threw a lavish party at his home before the 1988 Rose Bowl game, which Michigan State won, 20-17, over Southern California.

Clearly, Michigan State athletics have enjoyed rich exposure, much of it worldwide, because Earvin Johnson chose to play for the Spartans. Whether Michigan would have won a national title with him in the lineup is open for debate. And Michigan coach Johnnny Orr could only dream over the years of how his career might have been different if he'd have coached the player they called "Magic" instead of Jud Heathcote.

—*Tim Staudt*

When Magic and Bird Became Friends

It was in the summer of 1984 when Earvin "Magic" Johnson was asked to go to French Lick, Ind., to film a shoe commercial for Converse with longtime rival Larry Bird.

It was a junket Earvin was not looking forward to.

"We had a definite dislike for each other," said Earvin. "And I wasn't sure what to expect going to his hometown."

It turned out to be one of the best trips Magic ever made.

"We had a long break between shoots, and we just started talking," Earvin recalled. "It was amazing how much we had in common, and not just our love of basketball. We both grew up poor in the Midwest.

"We started laughing so hard over a bunch of different things, and we became good friends that afternoon. If it weren't for that commercial shoot, we wouldn't have become friends, and that would have been a shame.

"We helped change college basketball and pro basketball, and it's only right that we really got to know each other better."

Larry and Earvin were competitors to the end and drove each other to outwork the rest of the NBA. They had always respected each other, and now they were friends.

The two became so close that Earvin paid Bird the ultimate compliment by asking Larry to present him for induction into the Basketball Hall of Fame in the fall of 2002 in Springfield, Mass.

Magic Enjoys Signing

Four of us were sitting in the back of Starbucks in East Lansing trying to be as inconspicuous as possible.

But when one of the four ranks among the most recognizable faces in the world, it's difficult.

Ever the people person, Earvin "Magic" Johnson loves signing autographs and posing for pictures with adoring fans. *Photo courtesy of MSU Sports Information*

In East Lansing, it's impossible.

Shortly after our interview began, a line of four or five kids formed over Earvin Johnson's left shoulder. Almost instinctively, like one of his famous no-look passes, Magic turned around with a big smile and started signing autographs.

"What's your name?" Earvin asked in a kind way to reassure the nervous young lady.

He then wrote her a personal note and signed his name.

"I'm a people person," Earvin explained. "Some people shy away from it, but I enjoy signing autographs."

Earvin has two rules, though.

"I won't sign when I'm out with my family, and I won't sign when I'm on a date with my wife Cookie," he said. "Most people are very good about it."

"EJ The DJ"

For Earvin Johnson, life away from the basketball court did not consist of one party after another, as it does for some star players.

WKAR radio's Earle Robinson became a friend of Johnson's during his MSU days. Robinson hosted an urban music show on the university station called "Taking Care of Business." It was three hours of music, news and sports, and Robinson covered MSU home games to help him assemble his sports reports. Earvin was a frequent listener.

On Sunday nights, Robinson would spin discs as a disc jockey in East Lansing's most popular student night spot, Dooley's. Earvin and Jay Vincent occasionally stopped by, and Robinson let Earvin wear the headsets and "spin the discs."

He would get the crowd whipped into a frenzy and called himself "EJ the DJ."

If Earvin loved spinning records, cards were another leisure time passion. To this day, card games are a regular part of a return home to Lansing with about a dozen of his friends who have played a game called bid-whist since the college days. It is like bridge. You can play for money, but Earvin's games usually don't consist of financial remuneration, rather bragging rights among three tables of four guys each. The evenings would often last until two or three in the morning. Robinson's house was a perfect venue to meet away from the general public.

First Impression

Lansing Everett High School coach George Fox enjoyed having his brother Dick around the team in the mid-1970s during the Earvin Johnson era. Dick would volunteer to drive a van with team members aboard to various scrimmages, "so long as Earvin rides in my van," Dick laughed in recalling those days.

George had been telling his brother all about the new tenth grader about to make his Everett varsity debut in the early winter of 1974. George gushed over Earvin's potential, telling Dick that he was better than Holt's Jeff Tropf and that one day he'd play in the NBA. Tropf was an icon in Holt who went on to play at Michigan State and Central Michigan.

Earvin's first high school varsity game was at Lansing Waverly High School. He scored twelve points and fouled out, but Everett won.

"I wasn't impressed after all I'd heard," Dick Fox recalled. "I told George that he shouldn't tell anybody you think he's going to play in the NBA."

George used Dick's comments to motivate Earvin.

In later years, Earvin was seated at the head table at a banquet in Lansing when he spotted Dick Fox in the audience. He got up and made a beeline for the Fox table.

"He said to me, 'Hey Rich, do you still think I won't make it in the NBA?'"

It was all Earvin said and, while laughing, he turned and went back to the head table.

"Ma-Jeek ... Ma-Jeek"

Earvin and Cookie Johnson take five vacations each year, but their children only make four of them.

Each August, Magic takes his wife on a three-week junket to the French and Italian Rivera. They travel in style on a 180-foot yacht that has a crew of 12.

"I just love Italian food," Earvin said. "I've never had any food like it."

The Johnsons usually spend their time relaxing on the yacht or touring the quaint villages in both countries.

Just like in the states, Earvin is unable to keep a low profile.

"Ma-Jeek ... Ma-Jeek," holler the natives when his yacht anchors.

And when Earvin comes out on deck, they applaud and announce to the uninformed, "He plays the baskeets."

Every once in awhile, Magic has to pinch himself to make sure all this is real.

"Can you believe this?" Earvin asked Cookie once while the yacht cruised the Mediterranean Sea. "When I met you, I didn't have any money in my pocket. But I told you I'd take care of you."

He's lived up to that promise, and then some.

Some Neighbors

When Earvin Johnson Jr., grew up at 814 Middle Street in Lansing, his next-door neighbors were the Daniels and the Hornes. And living down the street was a buddy named Wayne Pruitt.

Fast forward to 2003.

Now when Earvin drives into his gated community in Beverly Hills, he may see Denzel Washington or Samuel Jackson or Sylvester Stallone—all of whom live on the same street.

Other neighbors include Eddie Murphy, Rod Stewart, Roseanne Barr, and Barry Bonds.

So do the neighbors get together often?

"There's a park where we take our kids to play, and we get a chance to visit with a lot of our neighbors there," Earvin explained.

Earvin's wife, Cookie, leads a Monday night Bible study group that includes Jackson's and Washington's wives.

What Sports Illustrated Jinx?

Earvin "Magic" Johnson has graced the cover of *Sports Illustrated* 25 times since vaulting into national prominence in 1976.

However, he defied the odds in his sophomore and final campaign in the green and white by appearing on *SI*'s college basketball issue in November—a full-color photo of him dunking a basketball in a tuxedo and top hat—and then being on the season-ending *SI* cover dunking over Indiana State's Bobby Heaton in the NCAA finals.

A *Sports Illustrated* representative said that Magic was the first player ever featured on the preseason cover of *SI* to lead his team to the NCAA crown.

It may have been too much pressure for an ordinary basketball player, but Earvin thrived on things like that and said, "It's an honor and I'm thrilled. But, it won't affect my play. I'm just going to try harder."

The *SI* preseason photo shoot took nearly a whole day in Jenison Field House, and Johnson was dead tired afterwards. "I'm more tired than if I had played basketball all day," he said.

His 25 appearances on the cover of *SI* is the fourth most ever for an individual.

Never a Doubt!

Mike Brkovich never doubted for a moment that Earvin Johnson would make it big in the National Basketball Association.

He was a tad surprised, however, that Magic had such a gigantic impact in his first year in leading the Los Angeles Lakers to an NBA title in 1980.

"It was kind of shocking to see Earvin jump center in that final game against Philadelphia and then pour in 42 points," Brkovich said. "I remember sitting in my dorm room and thinking that only a year ago we were playing together at Michigan State."

That Earvin would eventually lead the Lakers to five NBA crowns and leave the game as one of the game's all-time greats did not surprise the 6'4" guard from Windsor, Ontario, though.

"Earvin worked harder than anybody, had a pro body, had tremendous court awareness and played within himself," Brkovich said. "He was a smart player with a lot of basketball IQ."

Brkovich has fond memories of Earvin during his playing days, as well.

"He was good for me," Brkovich said. "I didn't have a lot of experience, and he always told me to get open and he'd get me the ball. He told me to shoot it and not worry about making it. It had a calming effect on me.

"Like most great players, he made everyone around him better. He made us all better. If you made a mistake, he'd let you know but it a positive way."

Brkovich hasn't noticed a change in Earvin, either, when the championship team has gotten together for reunions.

"He's still the same 20-year-old Earvin that I played with," Brkovich said. "He's always been a most gracious guy."

So Young, So Confident

Earvin "Magic" Johnson was only 19 years old when he had to make the most difficult decision of his life.

Would he declare for the 1979 NBA draft or come back for his junior season at Michigan State and, quite possibly, play in the 1980 Olympics?

"It's the hardest decision I ever had to make, much harder than deciding on what school to attend or whether to go pro last year," Johnson said. "I'm giving up a lot, but I'm convinced it's the right move for me."

All of the positives and negatives tumbled through Earvin's head during the two hours he sat by himself on the steps of Jenison Field House on Thursday, May 10. He had to declare by the next day.

"On the one hand, I had my teammates and fans and Coach [Jud] Heathcote," Johnson said. "And on the other, there was the money and the challenge of playing in the NBA. I did what I thought was best for me."

When it was pointed out to Magic that the Los Angeles Lakers (the team most likely to draft him) already had an established point guard in Norm Nixon, Earvin said, "There are two guards on a team, and we can either run together or he can sit down.

In the center of attention, as usual, Earvin Johnson brings the net down after Michigan State captured the 1979 NCAA championship. *Photo courtesy of MSU Sports Information*

"I'm going into the pros with the idea of being a starter, and I'm going after anybody's job I have to."

Mixed Emotions

Jud Heathcote has never been at a loss for words.

In fact, the stoop-shouldered Spartan basketball coach was at his best in the press conference following Earvin Johnson's decision to go to the NBA following his sophomore season at Michigan State.

"The Earvin Johnson era is over, but the aura stays with us," as Heathcote put it so eloquently.

Heathcote and Earvin had many long talks prior to his decision, so it didn't come as a complete surprise.

"I'm disappointed and yet thrilled for Earvin," Jud told the media. "I know he wrestled with the decision for a long time."

Asked what his initial reaction was to Johnson's announcement, Heathcote whimsically said, "I thought of two things, vomit or suicide, and I still may do both."

Magic Always Stole the Show

Since moving to Los Angeles in 1984, Darwin Payton has rubbed elbows with a lot of famous athletes and movie stars.

He's good friends with Denzel Washington and Jack Nicholson and has met the likes of Michael Jordan, Larry Bird, Tiger Woods, Julia Roberts, Oprah Winfrey, Muhammad Ali, Sylvester Stallone, Samuel Jackson, Janet Jackson, and the list goes on.

Does the personable manager on Michigan State's 1979 NCAA championship team ever stop and pinch himself to make sure this isn't a dream?

"You know when I pinch myself?" Payton said.

"It's to make sure that a kid from River Rouge is best friends with Earvin Johnson.

"Wherever we went, no matter who was there, everything revolved around Earvin. I honestly feel he's the greatest celebrity of them all … with the possible exception of Ali. He's the only one I wanted to ask for an autograph, but I didn't."

Still Waiting

Earvin Johnson and I sat down for a question and answer story for *The State Journal* in the spring of 1979 shortly after he declared for the NBA draft.

I asked him what it feels like to know that you'll be a millionaire soon?

"I really haven't thought much about it," Johnson told me. "I do think that I will be conservative, though. I'll get a nice car and buy some things that I need, but I don't want to go wasting my money, because I'd like to retire around 30."

"Retire at 30?" I questioned.

"I'm not going to spend my entire life in gym shoes," the Magic man said. "I want to do a lot of traveling and have a family by then. One of my goals also is to come back to Lansing, pick up golf and dog you at your own sport. That's a challenge for me.

"In fact, now that I'm going to have some money, I can even bet on it."

"It'll never happen, but how about $5?" I replied.

"You're on," Earvin said.

Well, he's now 44 and still spends as much time as possible in "gym shoes," and we haven't played our challenge match on the golf course.

—Fred Stabley Jr.

The Book That Barely Got Started

In the spring following Michigan State's NCAA championship, I decided to write a book about Earvin Johnson.

I jumped through all of the preliminary hoops, getting the okay from Magic and his agent Dr. Charles Tucker, and I went at it full blast.

I had some lengthy interviews with Lansing Everett High School coach George Fox and a number of Earvin's siblings. Fox turned over a box full of Earvin's recruiting letters that made for some fascinating reading.

I scheduled at least half a dozen interviews with Magic himself, and the big fella showed up twice—one time an hour late feasting on an ice cream cone. That never bothered me. Heck, I was a 31-year-old sportswriter at the *Lansing State Journal* and Earvin was already a national celebrity.

I knew nothing about writing a book, but I had a tremendously interesting subject and I was pretty excited about the whole thing. I even wrote much of the first chapter dealing with the early days of his basketball career at Main Street School and in the Johnson household with a rolled up pair of socks.

The two times Earvin did come to my house in Lansing were memorable, not only for the hour or so we spent rambling about his young life. It was a neighborhood happening.

I had three young children at the time, and because of them, I think every kid within a mile knew that Magic was scheduled to visit and they were ready.

He was gracious, as usual, and signed autographs.

My book plans came to a sudden halt when Dr. Tucker called me and told me that Earvin had been offered $50,000 for the rights to his story. That was quite a sum of money for a kid who grew up in a three-bedroom house with his parents and eight brothers and sisters.

Shortly thereafter, Magic signed the incredible contract (for those days) of $1 million a year for 25 years with the Los Angeles Lakers.

Of all the memories I have of Earvin at Everett and Michigan State, a couple of things stick out more than others.

It seems trivial now, but I remember checking in at a motel in Iowa City after a long trip from East Lansing. My daughter, Beth, was with me at the front desk when all of a sudden somebody jumped on my back.

It was the ever-playful Magic just saying "Hi."

And who will ever forget Earvin's first NBA game that was televised back to Lansing? Remember the look on Kareem Abdul-Jabbar's face when the 6'9" rookie jumped into the stoic seven-footer's arms when Kareem made a game-winning hook shot?

A diverse group of individuals, under the leadership of a fiery coach, united for one goal—the 1979 NCAA basketball championship. *Photo courtesy of MSU Sports Information*

It was a tad reminiscent of the Spartans' celebration following the regional final win over Notre Dame when Earvin and company rolled around the floor of Market Square Arena.

Jabbar's expression said it all: "Kid, we have 81 more regular-season games to go. Chill out."

Fortunately for Jabbar, the Los Angeles Lakers and Magic Johnson fans everywhere, he never did. He never lost his youthful exuberance, his zest for life or his love for the game he played like few others who ever laced up a pair of sneakers.

Thank heavens!

—*Fred Stabley Jr.*

Toasted

I was an average recreational basketball player, at best. But I loved to play and would do so almost every day during the non-golfing months of the year.

Lansing Everett used to have an open gym on Sunday mornings, and I had an open invitation from Vikings coach George Fox to come for a "run" any time I wanted.

I took George up on his offer one Sunday, and it so happened that Earvin Johnson was playing, too, along with a number of other outstanding players. I knew I was way over my head, but what the heck.

I was on Dr. Charles Tucker's team in one game and Earvin was on the other. We would only play to four baskets, as I recall, to get as many people on and off the floor as possible.

The game was tied at three apiece when Magic came busting out of the pack with the basketball. I was the only person back.

I think I know what Custer felt like at the Battle of the Little Bighorn. Even though it was one-on-one, I was outnumbered.

Earvin came flying across midcourt, dribbling the ball in his left hand and a sly grin on his face. He pulled up at the edge of the free throw line with a high dribble, and I closed to contend what appeared to be a jump shot.

As quick as you can say, "Blew By You," the big fella lowered his shoulder and ripped by me for the game-winning, left-handed dunk.

Earvin got a big chuckle out of it and Tuck chewed me out for not tackling him, anything to prevent the winning basket.

Sure, Tuck! I'm going to tackle Earvin, tear his ACL and become the biggest goat in Lansing sports history.

No thanks! Being toasted by one of the greatest basketball players to lace up a pair of tennis shoes was just fine with me.

—*Fred Stabley Jr.*

A Good Pass Must be Caught

Jud Heathcote had a tough time convincing Earvin "Magic" Johnson that the only good pass was one that was caught by a teammate.

"Earvin used to bounce a pass off an unsuspecting teammate in practice," MSU's head coach said. "He would insist it was a good pass, but I kept on pounding it into him that if the pass is missed, it's the passer's fault.

"It was Earvin's responsibility to get it to a guy when he could catch it, not when you think he should catch it. He became a tremendous passer, and 90 percent of his passes were the easiest ones possible, but he got credit and acclaim for the other 10 percent of blind and behind-the-back ones."

Johnson set the school record for assists with 491 in just two seasons and was still fifth after the 2002-03 campaign. His mark stood for seven seasons until Scott Skiles dished out 645 from 1983-86.

Where'd That Hook Shot Come From?

Earvin Johnson was always the last player to arrive at practice for Michigan State ... and the last one to leave.

"Earvin would come running in with his socks and shoes in his hands just a minute or so before 3 p.m.," Spartan mentor Jud Heathcote recalled. "I'd always say, 'E, we start at 3 p.m.' And he'd say, 'Coach, I'm here and I have a minute or two to spare.'"

He'd often have to wait for Earvin after practice, too, but this time it would be for him to leave.

"I'd be working at one end of the court after practice with Gregory Kelser on his post moves," Heathcote said. "Earvin would be shooting at the other end and holler that he'd like to come down, too.

"I told him he could play defense against Gregory, and Earvin said that he'd do that and then switch to offense. We spent a lot of time on his hook shot."

When Magic led the Los Angeles Lakers to the NBA title by scoring 42 points in the finals against Philadelphia—many of them sky hooks over Darryl Dawkins—the press asked him where he learned that shot. "From Kareem [Abdul-Jabbar]," Magic bubbled.

When Heathcote saw Earvin next he kidded him about it.

"Hey Coach, you know where I learned it and I know where I learned, but that's not what they wanted to hear," Magic said with a twinkle in his eye.

Mutual Admiration

E arvin Johnson and Jud Heathcote had their "moments" over the two years they were together orchestrating the fortunes of Michigan State basketball.

But when it was all said and done, and the Spartans finished with two Big Ten titles and an NCAA crown, both had nothing but good things to say about the other.

Johnson told the media following the NCAA championship tilt in Salt Lake City that Larry Bird was "the best player in college basketball."

Heathcote wouldn't buy it.

"Few people can thread a pass like Bird," Heathcote said. "But I still think that Earvin is the best all-around passer and player in college basketball today."

Johnson, on the other hand, was quick to defend and throw praise on his coach, who was often criticized for his quick temper and antics on the sidelines.

"The man's a winner. He wants to win and he's going to win," Johnson said. "He's a successful coach who cares about his players. He battles for his players.

"I hate when fans get the wrong impression about him and think all that he does is yell and holler. He's just a coach who gets caught up in the game and expresses his emotions.

"He's a perfectionist, and if you're a player you can't help but get your talent perfected under him. I'm going to miss him because we're real tight. We talked about a lot of things.

"Jud's like me in a lot of ways. I hate to lose and so does he. We both have a lot of pride and we're fighters. We don't think we will lose no matter what the odds.

"He made me a better player and I'm thankful for that."

And so are Spartans fans everywhere!

SPARROW
HEALTH SYSTEM

and

Physicians
Health Plan
of Mid-Michigan

**salutes
the MSU
Spartans!**